Teaching/Writing Resistance

Teaching/Writing Resistance

Women's Studies in Contemporary Times

Edited by

Panchali Ray and Shadab Bano

Orient BlackSwan

TEACHING/WRITING RESISTANCE: WOMEN'S STUDIES IN CONTEMPORARY TIMES

ORIENT BLACKSWAN PRIVATE LIMITED

Registered Office
3-6-752 Himayatnagar, Hyderabad 500 029, Telangana, India
e-mail: centraloffice@orientblackswan.com

Other Offices
Bengaluru, Chennai, Guwahati, Hyderabad,
Kolkata, Mumbai, New Delhi, Noida, Patna

First published by Orient Blackswan Private Limited 2024

ISBN 978-93-5442-908-8

039817

Typeset in
Minion Pro 10.5/12.75
by Le Studio Graphique, Gurgaon 122 001

Printed in India at
Thomson Press, New Delhi 110 020

Published by
Orient Blackswan Private Limited
3-6-752 Himayatnagar, Hyderabad 500 029, Telangana, India
e-mail: info@orientblackswan.com

Contents

Acknowledgments

This volume was conceptualised on the sub-theme 'Teaching Women's Studies', which was part of a National Conference on 'Women in a Changing World: Restructured Inequalities, Countercurrents, and Sites of Resistance' (2017) organised by the Indian Association of Women's Studies (IAWS). We are deeply grateful to the Executive Committee of IAWS (2014–2017) for first inviting us to convene the sub-theme and then pushing us to exert ourselves and put together a volume. Needless to say, without their encouragement and persuasion, we would not have trodden this path.

Apart from the insightful papers presented and the lively discussion generated in the conference room, certain other events gave rise to the need to re-examine women's studies and its future. The year 2017 proved tumultuous for scholars, researchers, and faculty members in India, who were facing very uncertain times. The Twelfth Five-Year Plan (2012–2017), which had released an unprecedented amount of funds to Women's Studies Centres (WSCs) across the country, was coming to an end; given the political climate, there was no surety of continuance of the relevant schemes. In 2017, the University Grants Commission (UGC) put out a notice that they would review WSCs to ascertain which centres were 'performing' and thus deserving of continuing funds. Under the leadership of the IAWS, the teaching, research, and student community of various centres petitioned the UGC, resulting in continuation and extension of funds on an annual basis. While there has not been any significant reduction of funds till date, the scheme is renewed annually and WSCs are under a constant threat of closure.

As editors, we were unsure whether we needed another book on 'women's studies' but as scholars and teachers of this fledgling discipline, we felt the moment keenly—we were not even sure whether women's studies, *as we know it*, would continue to exist by the time the book was out. There was an urgent need to address the pertinent issues and challenges facing the discipline amidst a time of major interventions in higher education. Thus, the book is not only informed by the theoretical interventions of presentations and discussions in the panels, but also the general tone and tenor of the conference, as well as important currents in collective action. We thank all those who presented papers and unfortunately, we could only accommodate a few; the loss is entirely ours.

The real push for the book came from the IAWS sub-theme coordinators' review meeting held in Ranchi in September 2017, and we are thankful to Indrani Mazumdar, Kiran Moghe, and Ritu Dewan for their encouragement. In particular, we thank Indu Agnihotri for her keen interest in our book and all her support. We take this moment to thank all women's studies scholars, researchers, and faculty who are struggling, across the world, in a system that systematically devalues them, all because they believe another world is possible.

Abbreviations

AMU	Aligarh Muslim University
AUD	Dr. B. R. Ambedkar University Delhi
BDU	Bharathidasan University
BU	Bharathiar University
CEDAW	Convention on the Elimination of All Forms of Discrimination against Women
CSSSC	Centre for Studies in Social Sciences, Calcutta
CSWB	Central Social Welfare Board
CSWI	Committee on the Status of Women in India
CWDS	Centre for Women's Development Studies
DU	University of Delhi
DWCRA	Development of Women and Children in Rural Areas
EIWIG	Economists Interested in Women's Issues Group
EWS	economically weaker sections
FRM	Feminist Research Methods/Methodology
GIDR	Gujarat Institute of Development Research
IAWS	Indian Association for Women's Studies
ICSSR	Indian Council of Social Science Research
IPC	Indian Penal Code
ISST	Institute of Social Studies Trust
JNU	Jawaharlal Nehru University
MHM	Menstrual Health Management
MHRD	Ministry of Human Resource Development
MIDS	Madras Institute of Development Studies
NDA	National Democratic Alliance
NET	National Eligibility Test
NGO	non-governmental organisation

RAWS	Regional Association for Women's Studies
SEDG	socio-economically disadvantaged group
SET	State Eligibility Test
SEWA	Self-employed Women's Association
SNDT	Shreemati Nathibai Damodar Thackersey Women's University
SPPU	Savitribai Phule Pune University
STEP	Support Team for Employment Promotion
TISS	Tata Institute of Social Sciences
WGFE	Working Group of Feminist Economists
WRPE	Women's Role in Planned Economy
WSC	Women's Studies Centre
UGC	University Grants Commission
UN	United Nations
UNDP	United Nations Development Programme
UNESCO	United Nations Educational, Scientific and Cultural Organization
UNICEF	United Nations Children's Fund
UPA	United Progressive Alliance
WHO	World Health Organization

Teaching/Writing Resistance
An Introduction

Panchali Ray and Shadab Bano

Women's studies has a very special history in India. The growth of this discipline was propelled both by women's movements as well as strands of intellectual thought that were committed to social, economic, and sexual justice. The interrelation between women's studies and women's movements, however, remains a complex one. Even as women's education acquired a central position within the agenda of anti-colonial struggles, with the country's independence, women's issues became invisible in the realms of politics and activism. The Nehruvian dream of a socialist society spawned complacency as well as the co-option of privileged and vocal women into state welfare programmes and charitable organisations. However, the 1970s witnessed a re-emergence of the 'women's question'. Both women's movements and women's studies were galvanised by two events: the Mathura rape case (1972) and the 'Towards Equality' report (1974), which successfully shattered the atmosphere of hope as well as complacency of the post-independence decades.

The emergence of radical women's movements, particularly in the 1970s and 1980s, that shared a contentious relationship with the State, also had the effect of pushing for a women's studies programme within the academic structure. The initiatives taken by the University Grants Commission (UGC) in the 1980s saw a streamlining of the conversations, debates, and sporadic efforts to establish the Women's Studies Centres (henceforth WSCs). The UGC's enunciation of guidelines for promoting women's studies reflected the concerns of women's movements and guided the setting up of WSCs in universities from the mid-1980s. Initially only four in number, by 2019, these centres stood at 163.

It is common knowledge that despite constitutional guarantees of gender equality, the country has not seen enough substantial changes towards this goal. Therefore, the establishment of WSCs that would tackle head-on the absence of research on women's issues was seen as the first step in addressing the massive inequality existing in the country. Initiated by the women's movements to counter the invisibility and marginalisation of women, WSCs set up within universities, research centres, and non-governmental organisations (NGOs) challenged the patriarchal structures of institutions, movements, and epistemology. Within a few decades, 'gendering disciplines/disciplining gender' became the totem pole around which revolved debates about the scope, nature, and ramifications of institutionalisation of women's studies as a discipline. Similar to women's movements, women's studies too shares a paradoxical relationship with the State. On the one hand, the 163 WSCs in the country today are funded by state governments and/or the UGC; on the other hand, part of the *raison d'etre* of women's studies is to challenge statist structures and spaces that historically invisibilised women. In the last few years, increasingly there have been ideological changes within the education system, leading to an attempt to restructure and redirect UGC-supported WSCs in ways that are a matter of concern.

Indian academia, right from colonial times, has been skewed towards 'skill-based learning' over 'general education'. Even in general education, a separation between the disciplines is endorsed, with a focus on education for 'development' of the 'nation', especially through the inclusion of science and technology over the social sciences and humanities. During the 1990s, with the introduction of Structural Adjustment Programmes, the State floundered in its developmentalist agenda which was increasingly reflected in higher education. In an era of globalisation, the move towards the privatisation of education has been accompanied by a concerted attack on public universities, particularly in the last few years.[1] The increasing irrelevance of the humanities, and also social sciences to a large extent, in the new corporate, vocation-centred universities has been particularly detrimental to WSCs. In an age when enrolling in higher education is increasingly about moving quickly through a curriculum streamlined to prepare students for a job, WSCs have no practical utility. As women's studies gradually expanded within academic spaces, the discipline found itself in a quandary: set up with a clear mandate of social transformation (it was often referred to as an arm of the women's movements), its institutionalisation demanded that it generate employment, whether in academia or elsewhere. Despite the ongoing struggles of women's studies to avoid marginalisation in academia, the developing situation is increasingly pushing it to the periphery; its greater vulnerability and lack of adequate State support have left the discipline to the vagaries of privatisation.

Besides the new trend towards privatisation, unmindful of the disparities and inequities working at different levels of education, the National Education Policy of 2020 poses a fresh challenge. Here, the constitutional objective of gender equality in education appears only peripheral and is incorporated more as an 'afterthought' (the category clubbed together with other socio-economically disadvantaged groups, or SEDGs). The overhauling of education intensifies already existing disparities and leads to further exclusion of marginal groups, particularly women students. Critical disciplines, like women's studies, now face the difficult task of questioning the State on these matters when access to education is being denied to most women students from unprivileged backgrounds, making the critical intervention of women's studies for gender parity all the more tenuous.

Apart from government defunding and increasing privatisation of education, as well as the New Education Policy (NEP) 2020, a greater challenge to women's studies, as with any radical curriculum, is being posed by the rapid growth and consolidation of right-wing forces and escalating caste violence, which affect public university campuses. Spaces that question, critique, and dissent find themselves under continuous attack as forums are being dismantled and teachers, researchers, and scholars are being questioned, witch-hunted, and arrested by fascist State powers.[2] With the introduction of reservations for economically weaker sections (EWS) in 2019, affirmative action that can fight caste-based exclusion in education has been further diluted. WSCs have already begun to feel the brunt as the threat of co-option looms large. This can be seen in the growing reticence/hesitation in raising issues for fear of backlash from hardliners; increasingly, events and talks are being called off in the face of threats as the establishment generally fears taking risks. Confronted with these real and perceived threats, there is a recoiling instead of reclaiming space. Besides, the impetus to digress, debate, and dissent no longer comes from the locations of advantage, and the onus is rather squarely placed on the already-weakened shoulders of disadvantaged groups (the Dalits, OBCs, and minorities) to question mainstream nationalism and its regressive policies. The everyday life within campuses, rife with casteism, homophobia, and misogyny, is questioned and challenged by women, Dalit, and other minority students who have gained some leverage with access to higher education. It is assumed that WSCs, along with other centres focused on social discrimination, would play a leading role in bringing about transformations within higher education. However, there appears to be both hesitation and fear in questioning patriarchal arrangements for women in the university, leading to a certain sense of disillusionment amongst students towards such enclaves of higher learning. The expectation that WSCs will play a more interventionist role in combating campus affairs that reinforce patriarchy has not been met.

The UGC established WSCs and women's cells in colleges/universities through different five-year plans, with agendas of not just teaching, research, and documentation, but also extension work, advocacy, and campaigning. While in many WSCs, UGC funds were used for programmes that had nothing or little to do with feminism, some WSCs were able to push for research, documentation, and advocacy that played a critical role in shaping policy in areas of employment, education, reservations, legal reforms, and reproductive and sexuality rights. However, the larger ideological framework of the Indian education system poses a dilemma for WSCs. For example, though the UGC has extended support to the WSCs, it emphasises workshops, training, and gender sensitisation programmes at the cost of teaching and research. The trends in the development agenda set by transnational think-tanks (World Bank, United Nations, and the International Monetary Fund) have seen a shift, with gender-mainstreaming as a core component in their various policies. However, the focus is not to question patriarchy, but to use a language of empowerment that reflects the country's aspirations to be an equal participant in the global order with developed nations. Nowhere has the appropriation of women's studies to suit the ends of the hegemonic social order been more apparent than the attempt at renaming 'women's studies' to 'women and family studies' in 2005. This constant push for WSCs to contribute to creating a pool of human resources—gender-sensitive professionals—who will take on the mandate of representing the country in a professional, knowledge-driven global economy means a fixation on a practical, utilitarian education. This, many feel, makes WSCs complicit with dominant social values and ideologies. Where increasingly higher education is being reduced to credentialing students for the marketplace, there is also a simultaneous NGOisation of WSCs.

The WSCs find themselves in a predicament. To retain funding from UGC, they have to offer a utilitarian education geared towards producing 'good citizens' for a country eager to find its place in the global order, at precisely that moment when the category of 'difference' has questioned the ideological and political foundations of women's studies. Difference has existed for many decades, and yet the homogeneity of the category 'woman' has never been under such siege. The explosion in post-structuralist feminist theories has questioned the very category 'woman', thus destabilising the subject of feminism and feminist politics. Theoretically post-structuralist feminists have dealt a bloody blow to the category 'woman', resulting in serious contestation of who constitutes the subject of feminism, and thus, the subject of women's studies programmes. On the ground, increasingly vocal queer and transgender people have been questioning the restricting and disabling category 'woman' and calling for a renaming of WSCs into gender and sexuality studies. While many argue that without an ontologically grounded subject, feminist politics will become redundant, it is also largely accepted that feminism cannot challenge anthropocentric definitions of knowledge without allying with post-structuralism. Given that some strands of feminism, particularly those instrumental in the ideological mandate of the emergence of the WSCs, are historically and theoretically rooted in modernism and reliant on a discourse of emancipation, it becomes even more vital to critically engage with theory to ensure that the larger mechanisms of exclusion do not get repeated in WSCs. This would require close readings of modernity to arrive at complex, multi-faceted feminist epistemology that critically engages with the question of the subject, particularly the Cartesian subject and its founding dichotomy of mind/body, without falling into binaries of modernism/post-modernism and practice/theory.

At this critical juncture in the histories of the WSCs, when feminist knowledge and analysis are making important transformations and the discipline is (re)thinking its fundamental tenets, threats of defunding destabilise any attempts to re-think and re-formulate. Women's studies was viewed with tremendous potential to bring about changes, and its achievements have been significant; however, a critical field that was expected to transform the existing structures of knowledge and establishment ultimately depends for funding on state agencies to run its centres.

The continuance of WSCs on the whims and fancies of political regimes has had the effect of disciplining the field. As we are all aware, only a few WSCs have been transformed into statutory departments by their respective universities and state governments; most continue to function with grants from the UGC. Recognising the achievements of the WSCs, the central government in 2011, under the Twelfth Five-Year Plan (2012–2017), granted unprecedented funds supporting research and teaching, which gave these floundering institutions a new lease of life. However, the euphoria was short-lived. A change in the government in 2014 brought with it a threat of discontinuing/reducing funds to all interdisciplinary spaces, such as Women's Studies and Centres for the Study of Social Exclusion and Inclusive Policy. Although in initial years there was no significant reduction of funds, the WSCs are kept under constant threat of closure. In 2017, the UGC put out a notice that they would review the WSCs to ascertain which centres were 'performing', and thus, deserving of continuing funds. Under the leadership of the Indian Association for Women's Studies (IAWS), the teaching and student community of the various centres petitioned the UGC, resulting in continuation and extension of funds annually. A yearly renewal, however, remains detrimental to both teaching and research as WSCs are never sure whether they will continue to receive grants in the next academic year. This profoundly affects teaching and research, as scholars and faculty members too are never sure whether their association with the centres will continue in the next academic session. In 2019, UGC issued a new set of guidelines that drastically reduced funding to WSCs, but later withdrew it in response to protests organised by the IAWS.[3]

One wonders whether it is a coincidence that just when the WSCs were expanding rapidly and moving beyond programmes of awareness and sensitisation—confronting their histories of exclusion, producing knowledge that fundamentally questions the dominant social order and its hierarchies, and challenging liberal agendas of a token inclusion of women (middle-class, upper-caste, heterosexual, able-bodied) within the social and economic order—that the UGC decided to restrict/withdraw funding. At the moment when WSCs are not just using intersectional analysis but also rethinking class, caste, race, ability, gender, and sexualities, not as pre-given or transparent categories but both synchronically and diachronically produced, there are threats of shutting down such spaces. Do WSCs now toe the governmental line of being merely spaces that equip women to fight for inclusion without questioning the gendered, classed, sexualised, racial/ethnic, and caste hierarchies to ensure continuity of funds? Has the relationship between the State and women's studies outlived its utility? Does the State now find the commitment of WSCs to new contours of emerging feminist knowledge useless to its project of education as central to the reproduction of capitalist economies? This essential condition of contradiction constituted the histories of the WSCs in this country and continues to affect their present form. How the 'official' and 'professional' spaces of feminist knowledge production negotiate and subvert such governmentalist agendas remains to be seen.

An Outline of the Book

Initially, women's studies made a crucial headway in countering the invisibilisation and marginalisation of women. With 'woman' as the subject of enquiry, feminist perspectives and epistemologies began to challenge received knowledge and intervene in traditional holds of academic disciplines. While feminist theory and methodology are used in all aspects of building women's studies programmes, there are considerable debates regarding the inadequacies of the universal, homogeneous category 'woman' as the subject of feminist studies and politics, or in the quest for a grounded subject. On the one hand, the efficacy of feminist thought and methods is contested by young practitioners and students who think this undermines the academic credentials of the field by making it too political. On the other, feminist politics in the present-day reconfigured global and national scenario is questioned for its lack/slackness of interventionist role or even for 'allying' with power. As issues of intersectionality and not just tokenising 'difference' are at the centre-stage, efforts to contest the exclusionary homogenising episteme, that of disciplining and institutionalisation, seek to foreground women's studies' fundamental commitment to critical knowledge. A set of eight chapters in this book offer diverse perspectives and raise crucial issues in contemporary debates challenging the monolithic understanding of the field.

Women's studies has come a long way from its initial foundation. The major interventions by women's studies need to be revisited if any attempt is made to grapple with contemporary issues and challenges. As the initial phase of women's studies and its contributions is often taken for granted, Devaki Jain in Chapter 1 traces the journey of women's studies from its early days in India, focusing on the efforts at knowledge-building and feminist intervention. Women's studies was conceived as the academic arm of the women's movement, where research was oriented towards action and knowledge built to intervene. Clearly as a perspective with goals for intervention, the accounts of the early struggles and success of women's studies were in the direction of building feminist epistemologies, gendering disciplines and public policies. As the early concern was to give visibility to women's experience and expose the structures of oppression, the field quite openly championed its political nature and contested academic neutrality. Interdisciplinarity at that stage meant bringing tools and frameworks from different fields to address women's oppression. The concerns of the discipline were not related to recognition in academia but to social action and change. The chapter foregrounds the tensions and issues in intervention, and the complications engendered by the emergence of intersectionality as plurality/diversity, with 'difference' becoming the hallmark of the women's studies movement.

The field of women's studies continues to be troubled by the category of 'difference', often pushing questions about various intersections to the margins. In Chapter 2, Mary John looks at the caste question in both feminist pedagogy and epistemology. She argues that knowledge of social movements, so crucial to women's studies, continues to be caste-blind, and despite classrooms becoming increasingly differentiated due to caste-based reservations, the issue is not central to pedagogy. John contends that one of the reasons for this is the evasion and blurring of caste in dominant histories of the social reform movement in colonial India. She revisits the campaigns and controversies in the nineteenth century, particularly the Age of Consent controversy of 1891, to provide a regionally differentiated narrative by comparing the case of colonial Bengal with western India. In Bengal, which is regarded as the centre of social reform, the dominant narrative of women's reform had been without any reference to caste or only with fleeting reference (in case of widow remarriage laws). In Maharashtra, Jotirao Phule and Savitribai emphasised both caste and gender; in contrast, matters relating to the girl child, such as marriage and education, were discussed mainly in gendered terms in Bengal. The emergence of Satyashodak Samaj in Maharashtra, which strove for an egalitarian society by resisting Brahmin hegemony and called for an abolition of Shudra and Dalit slavery, brought caste to the forefront. In her account, John traces the ways in which caste appears and disappears in existing histories of social reform and its possible fallouts for feminist pedagogy.

The dilemma facing women's studies today is a reflection of developments within the field as well as the consequences of macro policy changes in higher education. The increasing privatisation of higher education and the threat of reduced funding shows that policy is no longer in sync with the principle of education as a social good. And the insistence on curriculum across universities and institutions of higher learning being standardised and made uniform ignores social goals. The recent attacks on some of the best public-funded institutions, along with the attacks on plural, rational, and democratic ethos in the curricula, pose grave problems for the future of higher education in India and for a critical field like women's studies. In the face of these threats, concerns over institutionalisation of women's studies have gained greater urgency. While WSCs are trying to become statutory departments in their respective universities, thus making them 'safe' from vagaries of UGC funding, some fear that this process may lead to women's studies losing its critical edge by turning into a disciplined subject taught in a separate department. Thus, debates around interdisciplinarity take on a fresh urgency. Chapters 3 to 5 bring in the perspectives and concerns about interdisciplinarity and lack of academic rigour in women's studies, its potential to intervene, and other issues with departmentalisation and institutionalisation.

U. Vindhya in Chapter 3 deliberates on the body of knowledge, challenges in pedagogy, and the sites of resistance within the institution, and looks through this at the interventionary/transformatory potential of women's studies in higher education. She brings in her experience in teaching at a premier social sciences university (Tata Institute of Social Sciences) which actively encourages interdisciplinary and crossdisciplinary programmes. She examines whether the inclusion of women's studies in higher education is able to revitalise the university system, generate knowledge that facilitates greater inclusion of women in the higher education system, and in significant ways deal with reactionary forces. Women's studies as an interdisciplinary field is accepted and encouraged on account of its instrumental function—problem solving and professional preparation—but its transgressive and transformatory role has not been as readily accepted. The chapter looks at the different risks entailing feminist pedagogy as well as students' attitude and reaction towards the women's studies course and feminism in general. It also discusses the general perception of students wherein women's studies is considered 'soft' in scholarship and lacking in academic rigour. Vindhya particularly challenges the devaluing of feminist scholarship, which she sees as basic to women's studies pedagogy. She is critical of the very situation where students resent feminist perspectives and theories in the curriculum, not because they prefer 'neutral' and rigorous academic grounding but due to their discomfiture with feminism, to remain undisturbed by difficult questions.

Arpita Anand (Chapter 4) speaks of the difficulties women's studies faces not only vis-à-vis established disciplines, but also in terms of its recognition as a legitimate academic field. She lays out the existing challenges and emerging contradictions of interdisciplinarity within women's studies and how WSCs have functioned over the years. At the crux of the issue is the institutionalisation of women's studies and it being conferred the status of a degree-offering course, which has complicated the meanings of interdisciplinarity as understood and implemented in the field. Looking at the questions of interdisciplinarity through the experiences of five such WSCs that award degrees, Anand finds the meanings of interdisciplinarity complex and contradictory, complicated by its very identity-based object of study on one hand, and by the differing meanings of the 'lack of boundaries' and academic incoherence on the other. Anand argues that the academic rigour and neutrality of women's studies is weakened by the centring of feminist politics and use of feminist theory and methodologies. Besides, interdisciplinarity has not meant transcending disciplinary boundaries or developing academic content and methodology; rather it suggests a sense of openness to and a mix of disciplinary traditions.

This experience of interdisciplinarity as mainly institutional and not methodological accounts for the 'lack of core' and grounding in academic content and challenges the academic claims of women's studies. The 'lack of a boundary' defining the field may be celebrated as a strength, denoting institutional openness, or could be criticised for perceived incoherence. These ideas around institutional meanings of interdisciplinarity are nevertheless also shaped around concerns of employability of students, as much by the stage in degree pursued by the student (open at the entry level but quite closed-off at the level of research degree). For whatever concerns over the lack of boundaries that question the academic credibility of women's studies, there is now increased insistence on critical training in women's studies in order to teach women's studies as a proper discipline, or on closing of boundaries that would make the issue of interdisciplinarity far more complex.

Chapter 5, by Nithila Kanagasabai, speaks of similar concerns and anxieties over the institutionalisation of women's studies, its low status and lack of academic rigour, interdisciplinarity/'indiscipline', and understandings of the feminist project from non-metropolitan locations in Tamil Nadu. Despite the many challenges posed by institutionalised discipline and its incumbent emphasis on depoliticisation, NGOisation, and professionalisation, which limit the subversive potential of women's studies, the chapter brings out practitioners' everyday engagements and micro-negotiations with power structures and hierarchies of knowledge in academia. Kanagasabai raises the issue of intersectionality (here, among other identities, the local context and region enter feminist epistemologies), which challenges to the foundation of knowledge production and disciplinary paradigms produced at the metropolitan centres. Feminist politics at these centres are at the root of such negotiations and challenges. The possibility of transgression despite all odds is thus very much present within a commitment to women's studies. The engagement with feminist theory and action also addresses an older debate on the growing binary between activism and theory and the notion that over the years, women's studies is losing its 'originary' connection with the movement. Students and faculty concerned about the 'precarity' of the discipline and lack of academic rigour join various networks of women's studies activism and academia, while their keenness to foreground their own experience and that of their immediate community in the women's studies corpus marks their various initiatives towards 'disciplining' and 'decentring' of women's studies. These processes offer an ever-widening scope for transforming not only themselves but also the disciplinary boundaries and practices of women's studies.

The last set of chapters in this book examines the ruptures and repetitions in women's studies, the issues and concerns that continue to pose serious challenges. The issue of intersectionality has been a difficult one for women's studies/women's movements. Although the question of 'difference' was a basic premise to account for the multiple axes along which the oppression of women may be understood, it was by and large missing in larger feminist discourses/projects. This question of 'difference', forcefully foregrounded by hitherto disenfranchised groups, has not been able to transform knowledge production to the extent desired and continues to remain at the margins, with some token inclusion.

Chapter 6 discusses the fallacies of the dominant White feminist project that undermines and suppresses the struggles of Black women, women of colour, women from the Third World, etc. Sunera Thobani's problematising of intersectionality and marginalisation by dominant feminism in the West becomes useful in our context as it compels us to grapple with the complexities of our own locations. She contests the idea of solidarity in the women's movement in the West, which ignores or invisibilises differences. Thobani argues that the women's movement/women's studies not only failed to address intersectionality, but the concerns of disadvantaged groups were clearly not a priority for the movement; there being essential conflict of interest. Women's solidarity then is not merely 'bogus' or superficial but is a plank for the dominant within the women's movement/women's studies to further their agenda. In her analysis, Thobani raises concerns about the transformative potential of feminist politics and women's studies, where dominant White feminism allies with the State and weakens the anti-racist, anti-colonial movement of oppressed groups and nationalities.

Thus, while 'differences' were acknowledged by White feminists under the pressure of demands by oppressed groups, this failed to transcend mere tokenism. Rather, the dominant strand of Western feminism, in its discomfiture, has now found a common project with the State. This new ground was identified with the launch of the 'War on Terror', wherein Western feminists, by gendering Islamophobia and creating a binary between the 'secular-liberal West' and 'misogynist-oppressive Islamic world', have legitimised the imperialist war against Islam/Muslims. By presenting the figure of the Muslim Other as the most potent threat to women, sexual equality, and to queer and sexual minorities, they have blunted any emerging counter-hegemonic critique by whipping up fears about the 'dangers' posed by Islam. The hegemonic sway of this brand of White feminist discourse, and its impact on institutionalised women and gender studies, has increasingly marginalised the anti-racist and anti-colonial women's movement and overshadowed the struggles of the queer of colour and indigenous queer groups. This ensures, with greater force, the dominance of White feminism.

In Chapter 7, Panchali Ray asks: given the theoretical instability of the 'subject', can we envisage a discipline that is centred on the category 'woman'? She argues that once it was institutionalised within the university structure, feminism that was rooted in modernism committed to make visible and empower women, is unable to negotiate the tension that theory poses. She raises questions about the institutional politics of knowledge production to ask: What are the possibilities when radical thought is disciplined into a 'discipline', and once professionalised, can it continue to oppose the system to which it aspires to belong? While theoretically the category 'woman' does not obtain, the commitment of a women's studies programme to its historical legacy and roots makes it imperative to retain the category. Her critique of the institutionalisation of women's studies does not call for a dissolving of the centres, but rather, seeks to question the identity-based foundation of the discipline. She asks whether a women's studies programme that offers degrees is viable, given the tension between 'politics' and 'academics', and what ontological and epistemological contributions it makes in questioning patriarchal knowledge production. The pertinent question she raises is: 'can women's studies survive and adapt itself to the theoretical insights that question the very subject? Or has it outlived its political efficacy?' (see p. 160, this volume).

On the contrary, Chapter 8, 'The Future of Women's Studies, or Women's Studies "to Come"' argues that women's studies cannot have a fixed agenda. Instead it must be open to a future which cannot be anticipated. Thus, instead of arguing for or against a trajectory of what should/will be feminist theorising, WSCs should open themselves up to a future that is radical, unhinged, unfixed and, thus, impossible to foretell. It is this uncertainty that opens up the possibility of an undomesticated future, a move away from pre-determined agendas, thus making it impossible to reduce/tame feminism within institutionalised spaces such as the university. The commitment to a future that one cannot anticipate, an openness to a radical alterity is what will constitute a truly liberatory feminist programme.

Notes

1. See G. Arunima. 2017. 'Who's Afraid of Public Education?' *The Wire*, 3 March. Available at https://thewire.in/education/public-higher-education-privatisation (accessed February 2024).
2. See Human Rights Watch. 2020. 'India: Arrests of Activists Politically Motivated'. 16 September. Available at https://www.hrw.org/news/2020/09/16/india-arrests-activists-politically-motivated (accessed February 2024).
3. See *Newsclick*. 2019. 'Future of Women's Studies Hanging in the Balance, Yet Again'. 22 March. Available at https://www.newsclick.in/future-womens-studies-centres-hanging-balance-yet-again (accessed February 2024).

Part I

Disciplining Gender / Gendering Disciplines

Reflections on Possibilities

1 Unfolding the Story of Women's Studies in India

Understanding and Learning from Difference

Devaki Jain[1]

Understanding difference, explaining phenomena, chasing the causalities which not only create differences but keep differences embedded in situations of hierarchy or equality: this has been the journey of the women's studies movement. While women's studies or gender studies have now been included in the university's structure and are deemed to be a discipline, at its initiation in the 1970s (Sharma 2017) its ethic or overall concern was in generating enough knowledge and—to quote my dear partner in this arena, Vina Mazumdar—enough 'noise' to draw attention to injustice. Injustice, whether it is within the home or the public space, or even more importantly, in the information systems that feed into knowledge.

The birth of women's studies in India aimed to draw on empirical knowledge and influence public policy. The scholarly dimension or direction of women's studies came slowly but gradually with universities opening women's studies departments funded by the University Grants Commission (UGC). It was hoped that women's studies would lead to the gendering of various disciplines, such as sociology, economics, and politics, as they were being taught in the university, thereby transforming them.

To return again to the late Vina Mazumdar, one of the key actors in the birth of this discipline, at a national seminar on 'The Early Years of Indian Independence', held in August 1997 at Baroda, she said,

> The Indian Association of Women's Studies (IAWS) during its earlier years had to repeatedly face the conflict of identities among

> members. Were they to view themselves primarily as academics or as activists? Some felt the divide was unbridgeable, but many of us didn't agree. We were challenging not only established beliefs, stereotypes and myths about Indian women, but also the theory of academic-neutrality, and value-free, non-judgmental role of academic disciplines—social sciences in particular. (Mazumdar 1997: 4)

As Vina says, in the initial stages,

> we were all committed to 'change' [the] government's development policies, laws, institutions and procedures; behavioral and learning patterns; the education system; media, socio-cultural values and institutions, dominant mindsets of men and women who would not listen to women's needs, hopes, or despair and continue supporting (often unconsciously)—myths, that covered the reality of oppression—exploitation, humiliation, undervaluation, abuse, and fears—of all kinds of powerlessness, incapacities and failures. Our methods and areas of struggle could differ along with our skills, vocations and other reasons—but we were all parts of the same movement—with multiple identities, priorities, and preferences. (Mazumdar 1997: 9)

In that era of the 1970s, the concern was not only to get better information but also to participate in policy and programme. Thus there was a trend towards research for action and not research only for academic circles. There was a possibility of intervening in government plans and budgets as every ministry had set up an advisory committee of women to contribute to their programme.

It can be argued that the year 1975 and the declaration by the United Nations (UN) convening a world conference of women laid the foundation for many streams, including women's studies—ushering in a host of knowledge-based reports and interventions, both in policy and practice. However, there was a strong difference between the countries of the Global North or the imperialists, and the erstwhile colonies of the Global South.

The 1950s and 1960s were heady times, especially for the former colonies. There were struggles for freedom in several countries of the Global South to affirm their political rights. *Emancipation* and *liberation* were the words of the moment. Many of the women who emerged from these freedom movements became prominent leaders of social and economic struggles and also established national women's organisations.[2] Women's emergence as leaders, as part of the outcome of the freedom struggles, was a phenomenon characteristic of many nations in the postcolonial Global South. It was not a pattern in the colonising countries. They were instrumental in making early inroads for the inclusion of women's rights in charters like the human rights charter; they drafted the famous Convention on the Elimination of All Forms of Discrimination against Women (CEDAW) (Jain 2005: 87–89).

In 1973, the UN made a call to governments to prepare reports on the status of women in their countries, to be tabled at the first world conference on women organised in Mexico in June 1975. It was this report that led to the setting up of the famous Committee on the Status of Women in India (CSWI). Their report, *Towards Equality*,[3] set the benchmark for investigations into the condition of women in India, as well as provided a stimulus to the government to examine and take forward the proposals emerging from the findings. While many of the findings and recommendations of the report were contested from varied ideological perspectives, it was still the most progressive and fact-driven analysis at the time and was acclaimed worldwide for its wide-reaching dimensions.

What is however interesting to note, both as an Indian achievement, and as a reflection of the progressiveness of the 'old', are the recommendations of a committee that was set up by the Indian National Congress in 1939—pre-independence and pre-1975. In fact, the naming of the post-1975 period as the new, revolutionary women's movement, to distinguish it from the old movement characterised as conservative and reformist, may be misleading and needs rethinking, as I will argue from two illustrations.

A sub-committee called the Women's Role in Planned Economy (WRPE) was established in 1939 as part of the National Planning Committee to examine and make recommendations on women's role in the planned economy.[4] The report covered seven areas: civic rights, economic rights, property rights, education, marriage, family, and a range of issues including widowhood, caste, prostitution, rights to franchise, health, and leisure. 'The Report of the WRPE is worth our notice,' writes Nirmala Banerjee,

> If only because of its historical relevance: it shows that, even then, Indian women were by no means the icons awaiting male handouts as has been visualised by many scholars. In the final report, they did demonstrate a clear understanding of the issues at stake and an ability to put them in the framework of contemporary national and international thinking. They could also set up a network of working groups in different parts of the country in order to get region wise inputs. (Banerjee, quoted in Jain 2014: 1–12)

Its language and recommendations were so progressive, so 'modern'. For example, the WRPE Sub-committee insisted that the traditional vision of the man in front carving out new paths, and the woman trailing behind with the child in her arms, must be changed to 'man and woman, comrades of the road, going forward *together*, the child joyously shared by both' (Jain 2014: 33, emphasis added). Other major suggestions indicate the role of the state in the provisioning of equal opportunities, ensuring equal wage for equal work, and protection from dangers in employment (for instance, the threat of sexual exploitation and violence).

Perhaps the most radical recommendation of the WRPE concerned women's unpaid labour, both towards the family's economic activities and in the household. For the first kind, the WRPE recommended that the economic value of the work must be recognised and, in lieu of payment, '[s]he should have the right to claim all facilities given by the state to other workers' (Jain 2014: 5), for example, medical help, crèches, training, etc. As compensation for work at home—mainly housework—the women should get absolute control over a part of the family income, and also an inalienable right to a share in the husband's property. And the husband should pay on her behalf the contribution necessary for any social insurance scheme for workers that the state may introduce. There was also a suggestion that men should learn and practise household skills.

Currently, almost six decades later, the UN and feminist movements are calling for attention to care work and remuneration, revealing how far-sighted and progressive women leaders were, even sixty years ago, in India.

Further, many a time it was not the institution but the players who made the difference. J. P. Naik, as Chairman of the Indian Council of Social Science Research (ICSSR), led the stream that enabled research and the setting up of a committee in the ICSSR on women's studies. The encouragement provided by the ICSSR brought many of us into the field of women's studies.

The first National Conference on Women's Studies, held in 1981 at Shreemati Nathibai Damodar Thackersey Women's University (SNDT) in Mumbai, brought together not only scholars researching or writing on women/gender, but also many from activist networks and associations of women spread all over India. Since at that time there was no programme, as later designed by the UGC—where women's studies was established as a discipline, with financial support for a department or a centre of women's studies in universities—it was a gathering of those who were already engaged in uncovering the role of women in diverse spaces and in initiating and organising change.

The conference offered us an opportunity to get to know many others from our field who were otherwise scattered far and wide: in statistical institutes, in university departments, as teachers or as members of traditional women's organisations, or trade unions. However, not all were necessarily devoted to gender studies.

I had been engaged, from 1976–1977, along with my colleagues at the Institute of Social Studies Trust (ISST), New Delhi, in a time-use study to uncover the truth about women's economic participation. Our interest in uncovering the truth about women's economic roles emerged out of both the visual and the academic. Visual in the sense that one could not miss the picture, as one drove across different geographical zones of India whether by bus or car, or on our city roads, of women with their backs bent, working. Women were out in the fields, sowing paddy, pulling out weeds, picking tea leaves, gathering berries and other forest produce, grazing cattle and goats, and a host of other agricultural and non-agricultural activities. They were all engaged in what was obviously work that was adding to the gross national product. But when we looked at the national statistics on women's participation, it was abysmal as compared to men's participation. The National Sample Survey, 27th round, conducted in 1972–1973 by the National Sample Survey Office (NSSO), held that the female work participation rate was in the range of 30 per cent, compared to the male participation rate of more than 50 per cent.

I put in a proposal to the ICSSR to test the hypothesis that women's work participation is under-enumerated. I was able to recruit the partnership of the NSSO as V. M. Dandekar, its Chairman, could see the validity of my question. It took almost two years of fieldwork, living in the villages and recording what women, men, and children do on any day for over fourteen hours. The results of the study (Jain and Chand 1982), conducted with NSSO's participation, were convincing.

The data we put out challenged all the given assumptions about women's economic contribution, such as the idea that women were supplementary breadwinners. For example, we found that in assetless households, women were the primary breadwinners! Women and girls were working eighteen hours out of twenty-four. Boys played or went to school while girls cooked, cleaned, and carried. Girls were often breadwinners for the whole household amongst the poor.

Intriguing data like the low female participation rate in West Bengal was uncovered. Poor women and girls in West Bengal were working too, but 'undercover' in 'feminine' work—as domestic help or beggars rather than in the fields—often for non-monetary rewards. This study then led us into further research on women's economic roles and therefore to women workers in various occupations. Gradually, ISST came to be known for its intervention in economics.

We presented the findings of this ISST study at the first National Conference on Women's Studies (1981), where others involved in the field of women's work were also present. We then decided to form a network, and called it Economists Interested in Women's Issues Group or EIWIG (in order to be inclusive of men).

This group was encouraged by the Ministry of Labour as well as other ministries to examine and highlight the economic roles of women across sectors, including agriculture, industry, and even demography. EIWIG, with a membership of more than fifty persons, held four conferences over the next five years (1982–1986) on issues such as women in industry and agriculture, poverty vis-à-vis women, and the invisibility of women in statistics. Three of the seminars were: 'Women and Industry', convened by U. Kalpagam at the Madras Institute of Development Studies (MIDS); 'Women in Poverty', convened by Nirmala Banerjee at the Centre for Studies in Social Sciences, Calcutta (CSSSC); and a third convened by Pravin Visaria from the Gujarat Institute of Development Research (GIDR; the institute was at the time known as Gujarat Institute of Area Planning) in Ahmedabad. ISST was the energiser and helped raise funds from the Ministry of Labour and the Planning Commission for the seminars. These conferences took note of data on women's particular locations and issues arising from them, and also challenged how statistical data on these issues was being collected, compiled, and analysed. The four EIWIG seminars yielded another ISST volume, *Tyranny of the Household* (Jain and Banerjee 1986), drawing attention to all aspects of women and their work (Jain 2003: 268).

Women's work often increased as a result of 'development' interventions without any corresponding increase in either income or convenience. Men preferred to remain idle rather than work for poor wages. An invitation to give the Padmaja Naidu Memorial Lecture (Jain 1982) gave us a chance to wave these facts from the rooftops, so to speak, to challenge the social scientists. On what basis were the statisticians counting workers and their work? Women from assetless households had higher work participation rates than men from the same households. What was this 'sociological family' they were talking about? What were all these tracings of kinship organisations in India and their rules and regulations? These were fragmented *non-families* in which women battled for life (Jain 2003: 263).

This differentiation between men and women amongst the poor, now known as gender differentiation, became the crux of all the research and advocacy of ISST and many other Women's Studies Centres. This uncovering of women within the poverty sets as a 'class' by themselves was of crucial importance to the journey as it challenged political ideology apart from economic programmes (Jain 2003: 264).

The second entry point was to look for situations in which women were the predominant workers, and where their engagement in that work was recognised and organised in order for them to improve their economic and social strength. This search was initiated because of news of the Self-employed Women's Association (SEWA)[5] as an organisation of self-employed workers—workers who were in the informal sector, but whose unionisation had transformed their negotiating power. At that time SEWA was the women's wing of the Textile Labour Association, a strong trade union presence in Ahmedabad. An ICSSR-funded case study of SEWA led to a search for similar organisational experiences of large masses of women. A 'survey of India', looking for such 'successful endeavours' led to the book *Women's Quest for Power* (Jain 1979).

The book and its design opened up a style of writing case studies—drawing from ground-level experience, creating a primary data profile from an on-the-spot household survey, followed by narrations that brought in the voices of women. It also established another proposition, namely that poor women were able to identify spaces where they could eke out a livelihood, even if only at survival level, but providing backward and forward linkages (such as organisation, market intelligence, and access to raw materials or wholesale goods through collective purchase) could enhance their income by many times. Thus, there emerged a critique and a revision of the mode of developing income-generating projects for women: such projects were the primary mode of intervention at the time and were supported by the government, and also by agencies like the Central Social Welfare Board (CSWB), United Nations Children's Fund (UNICEF), and Development of Women and Children in Rural Areas (DWCRA). The suggestion, then, was that the survival strategies of poor women can teach development design (Jain 2003: 264).

Thus began the search for groups or clusters of women who were already in a particular occupation, and the effort was to expand that space. This in turn led to the Government of India's national programme called Support Team for Employment Promotion (STEP). The experience also led to the birth of *Mahila Haat*, a market facilitating window for women producers, at ISST. The idea here was to start with the traditional *haat*s as these were viable marketplaces where the turnover of trade was greater than all the modern markets.

Here, women were often able to sell what they produced since the idea for what was to be produced came from the marketplace itself (Jain 2003: 264).

In 2004, when a new government was formed by the United Progressive Alliance (UPA), the friends and associates of EIWIG considered starting an economic policy watch as a way of developing a new lobby or voice comprised of women economists. The Eleventh Five-Year Plan (2007–2012) was being designed at the time and this loose network considered engaging with it to foster a knowledge-driven gendering of public policy. The woman member of the Planning Commission, Dr Syeda Hameed, was eager to bring the woman's question into the mainstream, rather than treating it as an issue only requiring welfare and handouts. This led to the Planning Commission constituting an additional expert group, namely the Working Group of Feminist Economists (WGFE). Members were drawn from the earlier EIWIG, as well as other groups, to review the sectoral chapters of the Eleventh Plan through a gender lens.

Beginning with the approach to the plan, and the first chapter which was about inclusive growth, the WGFE engaged with chapters on sectors like infrastructure, industry, agriculture, education, environment, and health. The feminist economists provided facts, critique of the draft, and ideas for change. The Group was able to make a difference to how women and their roles at the lower rungs of the economy were perceived and understood, and these women were renamed as growth agents. The Group critiqued the approach to the Eleventh Plan for its limited view of 'inclusive growth'—namely the notion that 'inclusion' was an add-on to 'growth' rather than intrinsic to the growth process itself. In particular, the draft had insufficiently acknowledged women as economic agents who directly contribute to growth, rather than being recipients of welfare or development.

This work also involved recognising that the nature of work in which women are concentrated has implications for city planning and the use of space, for example, to allow home-based work, street vending, and to integrate waste-pickers into municipalities. Engaging with the draft chapters, the Working Group established the primacy of women and their work in India's growth achievements, and argued that the planning processes and methods exhibited an inadequate awareness of these facts. The value of this initiative was that it argued for moving beyond a special focus on women, usually a chapter on 'Women and Child', to understanding women as growth agents in all sectors across the political economy of India. Thus, the major shift through this initiative was to move the engendering of public policy into the macroeconomic space (Government of India 2010). The uncovering of gendered difference in social and economic fields was useful in influencing policy and programme at the national level. This idea was then picked up by state planning boards.

The scholarly dimension of women's studies came slowly but gradually. With universities opening departments, and the UGC providing funds for WSCs, this aspect has grown—perhaps at the expense of learning from the ground to shift policy and programme. However, the other aim of the women's studies initiative was also to 'penetrate' the syllabus and curriculum of various subjects in university education. For example, for economists, the idea was to ensure that courses in economics, whether it was statistics, public finance, or macroeconomics, would contain essays and lectures that would show the importance of weaving gender into any argument or hypothesis. Thus, ideally the aim was to change the core reasoning in economic theory, apart from informing changes in the database. Similarly, in other subjects like sociology and politics, the effort was not merely to have readings on women within these subjects, but to critique definitions and propositions on causality.

In this chapter, I suggest that the requisite leap has not quite taken place. Although women's studies does weave new knowledge and understandings of difference, inequality, and geography, the critical entry into the knowledge system is yet to take place.

The syllabi and reading lists in many WSCs across universities still seem to be greatly influenced by what we call the 'West' or 'the Western academic world'. There is a case to be made for theorising from empiricism, from knowledge gained in the field, and using those theories to intervene in theory as it is taught across departments. I also suggest that in the present times, women's studies in India, instead of being 'outward-looking' has become 'inward-looking', thus disconnecting to a great extent from the public space.

Women's studies in other countries have also had many internal debates on identity, language, and integration. For instance, in the USA, a central focus of the internal discord was the question of what the prevailing definition of feminist theory should be within women's studies programmes. A. E. Ginsberg (2008) listed 'Liberal feminism, radical feminism, psychoanalytic feminism, cultural feminism, Marxist feminism/socialist feminism, standpoint epistemology, modern and postmodern feminism, and postcolonial feminism' as just a few of the dominant theories that practitioners and theorists have engaged with in the last forty years (ibid.: 13). To add to the stress of these different, often opposing, viewpoints, some women's studies practitioners rejected *all* theories, arguing that the use of theory itself was a hallmark of the traditional male curriculum and that many feminist theories can be difficult to translate into practice, therefore alienating women outside the academy (Crouch 2012).

Whether a practitioner supported a particular feminist theory or no theory at all, prominent publications and academic tensions of the 1980s focused on '[t]he overall question of what unites and defines the category of women…can we talk about "women" as if they are a cohesive category?' (Ginsberg 2008: 19).

As women from underrepresented identities realised that the women's studies programmes of the 1970s and early 1980s did not adequately represent them or their perspective, they developed their own movements and fields of study to give voice to their experiences. Black women's studies programmes began with the intention of placing women of colour at the centre of women's studies and changing the curricula to include research by Black women authors and Black feminist literary criticism. The success of Black women's studies inspired the development of several other fields of study that contributed to the transformation of women's studies, including American Indian Women's Studies and Asian Pacific American Women's Studies. The introduction of these perspectives 'changed the face of feminist scholarship, making it intellectually irresponsible to talk about "woman" as an undifferentiated universal category' (Kennedy and Beins 2005: 4).

I have lost touch with the women studies centres and universities in India, though I have met students who obtained their MA and MPhil. in women's studies from various campuses. It would be of interest to me to know if extraordinary scholarly outputs have come out of the second or third generation of women who have participated in these centres and whether we have made a leap from the outside to the inside.

Notes

1. I am grateful to Neha S. Chaudhry for her assistance in writing this chapter. She holds an MPhil. in women's and gender studies from Ambedkar University, Delhi. I am also grateful to Shaista Nasreen, who holds a doctorate in women's studies from Jamia Millia Islamia, New Delhi, for her assistance in rewriting and making corrections for this chapter.

2. For example, the National Federation of Indian Women founded by Aruna Asaf Ali and the All India Women's Conference founded by Kamaladevi Chattopadhyay. Anasuya Sarabhai founded the Textile Labour Association, India's oldest and largest union of textile workers, in 1920. Durgabai Deshmukh established the Central Social Welfare Board in 1953. Sarojini Naidu went on to preside over the Asian Relations Conference in March 1947. Kamaladevi Chattopadhyay struggled for the township of Faridabad on the outskirts of Delhi. Sucheta Kripalani became the first woman to be elected as the Chief Minister of a state (Uttar Pradesh) in 1963.

3. The full report is available at https://feministlawarchives.pldindia.org/category/towards-equality/towards-equality-towards-equality/ (accessed 5 April 2018).

4. The Sub-committee to discuss women's role in the planned economy was formed on 16 June 1939 to 'deal with the place of woman in the planned economy...' ranging from family life, employment, education to social customs that prevent women's participation in the economy. See K. T. Shah's Introduction to 'Woman's Role in Planned Economy' (1947: 27). The chairperson of the committee was Rani Lakshmibai Rajwade, and the committee included prominent women of that time: Sarla Devi, Vijaylakshmi Pandit, Begum Zarina Currimbhoy, Sarojini Naidu, Durgabai Joshi, and Muthulakshmi Reddy.

5. See http://www.sewa.org/ (accessed October 2023).

References

Crouch, Betsy. 2012. 'Finding a Voice in the Academy: The History of Women's Studies in Higher Education'. *The Vermont Connection* 33 (1): 16–23.

Ginsberg, A. E. (ed.). 2008. *The Evolution of American Women's Studies: Reflections on Triumphs, Controversies, and Change*. New York: Palgrave Macmillan.

Government of India. 2010. 'Engendering Public Policy'. Report on the Work of the Working Group of Feminist Economists during the Preparation of Eleventh Five Year Plan 2007–2012. Planning Commission.

Jain, Devaki. 1979. *Women's Quest for Power: Five Indian Case Studies*. Delhi: Vikas Publishing House Pvt. Ltd.

______. 1982. 'Indian Women: Today and Tomorrow'. Padmaja Naidu Memorial Lecture, Nehru Memorial Museum and Library, Teen Murti House, New Delhi.

______. 1996. 'Valuing Work: Time as a Measure'. *Economic and Political Weekly* 31 (43): 46–57.

______. 2003. 'Building a Service Station Brick by Brick: Institute of Social Studies Trust'. In *Narratives from the Women's Studies Family: Recreating Knowledge*, Devaki Jain and Pam Rajput (eds): 259–286. New Delhi: SAGE Publications.

______. 2005. 'Questioning Development Paradigms, 1976–1985'. In *Women, Development and the UN: A Sixty-Year Quest for Equality and Justice*. Bloomington and Indianapolis: Indiana University Press.

______. 2014. 'Understanding Leadership: Lessons from Women's Studies Movement'. *Interrogating Women's Leadership and Empowerment, IIC Quarterly* 39 (3 and 4): 1–12.

Jain, Devaki, and Malini Chand. 1982. Report on a Time Allocation Study—Its Methodological Implications. Available in the digital library of the Institute of Social Studies Trust (ISST), New Delhi.

Jain, Devaki, and Nirmala Banerjee. 1986. *Tyranny of the Household: Investigative Essays on Women's Work*. Delhi: Vikas Publishing House Pvt. Ltd.

Kennedy, E. L, and A. Beins (eds). 2005. *Women's Studies for the Future: Foundations, Interrogations, Politics*. New Brunswick, NJ: Rutgers University Press.

Mazumdar, Vina. 1997. 'Perspectives on Independence through Women's Eyes'. National seminar on 'The Early Years of Indian Independence', August, Baroda.

Shah, K. T. 1947. 'Woman's Role in Planned Economy, Report of the Sub-Committee'. *National Planning Committee Series*. Bombay: Vora & Co., Publishers Ltd.

Sharma, Ashmita. 2017. 'Why Women's Studies? Contemporary Relevance and Future Discourse'. *Economic Political Weekly* 52 (21). Available at https://www.epw.in/journal/2017/21/web-exclusives/why-womens-studies.html (accessed October 2023).

2 Women's Studies and the Caste Question

Revisiting Social Reform and the Making of Indian Culture

Mary E. John

Women's studies in India was born in the 1970s and has been frequently linked with the publication of the *Towards Equality* Report of 1974 (Sharma and Sujaya 2012) on the one hand and with the rise of a new phase in the women's movement in the early 1980s on the other. The period of the 1970s and 1980s can perhaps be called a time when social movements like the women's movement and those within higher education were overwhelmingly 'caste blind'. Discourse on caste was folded within analyses of poverty and development (and often not even very visible there), a staple within the sociology syllabus, and did not figure as a public political issue except perhaps in specific regions such as Maharashtra and Gujarat when rocked by anti-reservation campaigns during these years. But even here, Sharmila Rege, trained in sociology and a women's studies pioneer in her scholarship on caste and gender, had this to say in her introduction to *Writing Caste, Writing Gender: Narrating Dalit Women's Testimonios* (Rege 2006):

> Looking through the long list of recently published translations of dalit writings, mainly life narratives, one is tempted to think that a rupture of kinds may be taking place in our teaching and learning of caste studies. Two decades ago, for many of us studying social sciences in regional universities in India, caste was considered mainly a 'sociological' subject. Undeniably caste was central to the courses on Indian society, which, however, were then neatly compartmentalised into social structure and social change over two academic terms.... Writings on/by Phule, Ambedkar, Periyar

> were not on the list of readings and most of us remained largely ignorant of the *abrahmani*/non-brahmanical perspectives on caste. (Rege 2008: 452–453)

Rege goes on to remark that in spite of all the subsequent ruptures, such as the anti-Mandal protests and organising by Dalit women, which posed serious challenges to the women's movement and feminist scholarship, 'except for a few notable exceptions, women's studies scholars did not seriously engage with dalit feminist critiques.... Reflections on caste in the curricular protocols of women's studies have been even rarer' (ibid.: 455). As her legacy so abundantly attests, Rege's lifelong commitment was to create pedagogical materials that would empower subaltern students and promote interpretative and political engagements with caste.

In my experience as an upper-caste teacher over the last decade, the situation in women's studies has not changed palpably, even though the work of scholarship has grown. Most of the time, within a heterogeneous classroom, we end up addressing 'caste' by treating it as a problem of 'weak' students or of a language divide.

In this chapter, I offer one way of addressing the question of caste in the teaching of women's studies by revisiting a well-known and much-studied slice of colonial history. The women's movement in India is seen to have its roots in the social reform period, wherein the story of colonial Bengal has been much more prominent than, say, that of the western region, or the south. To put this somewhat differently, the history of social reform has been contained within an unmarked national frame, one that was primarily shaped by events and struggles in colonial Bengal. One of the consequences of this framing is that the dominant narrative of the social reform of women has been told as a story that did not require reference to caste in any significant way. It is only with a new understanding of the struggles for social justice led by Jotirao Phule and Savitribai in mid-nineteenth century Maharashtra that it has belatedly become clear that the story of women has to be one of both caste and gender, and that this was true for all women, whether 'high' or 'low'.

I use the subject of child marriage, which was at the heart of what was seen to ail Indian society, to make my arguments. The following account revisits the first campaigns and debates in the nineteenth century, leading up to the Age of Consent controversy of 1891, by providing a regionally differentiated narrative. In so doing we can perhaps better appreciate the ways in which the story of the social reform of the woman-child leads a kind of double life. On the one hand, it can be told as a story that is basically about women, but when we shift the locus regionally, we see that the very same set of demands have to be rendered as an account of both caste and gender. Moreover, by the end of the Age of Consent controversy, with the rise of militant nationalism, caste/gender gets dissolved into a preoccupation with women's place within an embattled national culture. From the vantage point of the present, such a reading may make students and teachers alike more sensitised to the politics of caste in a context where our caste blindness has found new life under the debilitating conditions of a violent, majoritarian Hindutva politics. There are many strands, events, and famous men (and thereafter many women) associated with the history of child marriage in colonial India. Feminists and scholars of social history have been quite active since the 1970s in making some of this history more widely available. School textbooks across the country since at least the 1960s feature icons from colonial Bengal like Raja Rammohan Roy and Pandit Ishwarchandra Vidyasagar, while the achievements of Jotirao Phule in the western region of colonial Maharashtra are only now beginning to be better known.

Beginnings in Colonial Bengal

The social reform period stretches from the late eighteenth century to the first decades of the twentieth century. Most historians begin their explorations of this period with the extensive debate over the practice of sati or widow immolation in colonial Bengal between the 1780s and 1830. According to Lata Mani's (1989) influential account, if one looks closely at the three decades of controversy over whether and how to ban sati, the woman herself does not feature in the debates that unfolded between British colonial officials, Indian pandits, and reformers like Rammohan Roy, which are instead about whether the practice of sati is to be found in ancient religious scriptures. This was a debate about religion as scripture and not about women. The significance of Mani's study was to replace linear accounts of modernisation or the emergence of women's empowerment with the frame of a colonial discourse, which relied on Hindu scriptural injunctions for any consideration of reform.

While sati was a very specific phenomenon undertaken by small numbers in certain parts of Bengal and to a lesser extent elsewhere (gaining hugely in global publicity because of the extreme violence associated with it), the less sensational practice of ritually enforced widowhood was much more widespread, certainly amongst upper castes. A very significant number of women in the Indian population were found to be widows, that is, they were seen as no longer having the protection of a husband. As Janaki Nair has put it, the law against widow immolation may have 'saved them from the pyre, but condemned them to a living death' (Nair 1994: 61). Here, it was the child widow who grabbed the attention of the reformers, especially those who may have never left their natal homes or where the marriage had not been consummated. Widowhood was not just very common, but practically speaking a phase in the life cycle of women whose husbands were older than them. In several instances where such men died early, the wives left behind were little more than children. Brahminical laws decreed that widows remain chaste. According to another commentator: 'Irrevocably, eternally married as a mere child, the death of a husband she had perhaps never known left the wife a widow, an inauspicious being whose sins in a previous life had deprived her of her husband, and her parents-in-law of their son, in this one' (Carroll 2007: 114–115).

One strand in the history of child marriage in India therefore begins with the figure of the child widow. Reform led by Ishwarchandra Vidyasagar in Bengal took the form of a demand for the legal possibility of her remarriage. Pandit Vidyasagar was equally concerned with child marriage and girls' education, urging in 1850 that girls be at least eleven years old for marriage and boys eighteen years old. In 1861, the British declared in the new Indian Penal

Code (IPC) that sexual intercourse with a girl below ten years of age would be considered rape. While laws for widow remarriage were first proposed in 1837, it took till 1856 for them to be passed. Questions of caste make a somewhat fleeting entry here. For example, one of the reasons for the initial opposition to widow remarriage was that 'such a law would lead the Hindus of upper castes and classes to be confused with the inferior castes and tribes among whom remarriage was common' (Nair 1994: 60). Others have pointed out that this law, for all its positive intentions, had negative effects on precisely those castes and communities for whom remarriage had not been an issue. This is because the new law introduced certain provisions that effectively curtailed the more open remarriage practices among these non-elite castes (Chowdhry 1993; Carroll 2007).

In retrospect, it may appear odd that the very practice of child marriage achieved some measure of acknowledgement first via its tragic outcome in the significant presence of child widows. On further reflection this is quite understandable, since child marriage per se had yet to attain the status of a problem. But since the widow had lost the source of protection sanctioned within patriarchy, she could be viewed as an abject figure, isolated and deprived for no fault of her own. The child widow thus invited considerable sympathy if not intervention, and the younger she was, the greater the identification with her plight. It took almost a century of social reform for child marriage itself to enter the fray of legislative action, as the nineteenth century came to a close.

A much larger preoccupation that spanned several regions of colonial India, more so in the south, was that modern childhood was most closely entwined with ideas of education and schooling. This was true elsewhere too, but what may be unique to the Indian situation is the influence of colonial education on a girl or woman's age at marriage. In the Indian context it was education that had a decisive impact on marriage, including when it took place, whereas in other parts of the world it was work. More attention must be paid to the realm of education and its ramifications to understand changes in the institution of marriage. Matters relating to girls' education were for a long time as controversial as the more publicly contested issues of marriage and widowhood.

In his study of western education in colonial India, Sanjay Seth has questioned why the subject of female education was a matter of constant discussion when the actual numbers of girls and women in education was so miniscule, and 'in staggering disproportion to the number of girls affected' (Seth 2007: 129). As late as 1882 there were just six girls in college, over 2,000 in secondary schools, and 124,000 in mixed primary schools, mainly in the Presidencies of Bengal, Madras, and Bombay. He goes on to say that by the end of the nineteenth century, there was in fact widespread agreement in favour of the idea of women's education, but this did not result in a significant increase in numbers since women were burdened with being the bearers of Indian culture for the incipient nation (Chatterjee 1989), and a western education was inappropriate for such women. These so-called obstacles however run considerably deeper once their links with marriage are brought into the picture.

In the early years of social reform in the nineteenth century, the education of girls was not on the colonial agenda. The British were concerned with using western education as a training ground for Indians who could be incorporated into the lower rungs of the administrative system, with English-educated Indians being preferred for government appointments. Such Indians—it should be obvious—were entirely men. Wealthy Indians themselves took the first steps before the government stepped in, beginning with the establishment of the Hindu College in Calcutta in 1816. The first teachers to explicitly approach girls in their homes were missionaries or, more commonly, the wives of missionaries. Geraldine Forbes (1986, 1998) has discussed the specific interest in teaching women and girls, which led to their opening the first girls' schools where native Christian women were also brought in as school teachers. Thus was established the Calcutta Education Society for the promotion of girls' education, though families were initially hesitant to send their girls to school. Even the patronage of Indian gentlemen and the presence of Brahmin pandits on the staff did not suffice. Note that this narrative, which underscores the fundamentally controversial nature of education for girls, does not require much further elaboration about caste and caste differences. This changes when the locus of the narrative shifts to a different region.

A Different Framing in Western India

There has been as much scholarship, if not more, on western India compared to the better-known Bengal example when it comes to social history more broadly, and questions relating to women's reform more specifically. However, for reasons that probably have to do with Calcutta being the seat of colonial power, Bengal has retained its dominance in histories of social reform. One of the interesting aspects of scholarship on the region that now falls broadly within the state of Maharashtra is that accounts of reform foreground structures of caste as much as those of gender when discussing what ails Indian society. It is instructive to contrast otherwise very similar themes pertaining to women's status—the home and gender segregation, purdah and public exclusion, the public/private dichotomy, marriage and bearing children and so on—in works dealing with Maharashtra (Chakravarti 2005; Deshpande 2002; Kosambi 2007; O'Hanlon 2014) with those on Bengal (Chatterjee 1993; Sarkar 2001; Sarkar and Sarkar 2007; Sinha 1994). It is immediately clear that the problems of women in a region like Bengal are discussed in largely gendered terms (at least when it comes to its *bhadramahila* middle-class, upper-caste woman), whereas in Maharashtra the story can only be told through the working of gender and caste together, and for all women, whether 'high' or 'low'.

One early sign of this difference can be vividly seen in the belated discovery of the pioneering efforts of Jotirao Phule and his wife Savitribai. There is now a burgeoning literature on Phule, including some translations of his writings, though equal attention has yet to be paid to the extraordinary life and work of Savitribai, who is unfortunately folded in as a 'wife' into accounts of the man who was the first to be called a Mahatma. Unlike Raja Rammohan Roy or Pandit Vidyasagar, who came from upper class and caste backgrounds, Phule was born into an agricultural caste, a Shudra. Thanks to having a father who was a building contractor, he was able to complete a school education. Phule's translator G. P. Deshpande makes the interesting comment in his introduction that while other reformers were influenced by 'the rather weak English branch of European liberalism' (Deshpande 2002: 3), Phule had read Thomas Paine's *The Rights of Man*. Phule established a school for *Shudr-atishudra* (Shudra and Dalit) girls in 1848, the first of its kind anywhere in India. His father was shocked and, fearing a backlash from the upper castes, threw both him and his new wife out of the house. Phule continued undeterred with other sources of support, including from missionaries and the British state. Another school was opened in 1851 for girls from all castes. Many of his other actions, such as throwing open the family well to those deemed 'untouchables', were equally revolutionary, and not just for his time. Interesting, too, is that the terminology used by him and his followers was not that of social reform but rather of social justice. Phule's agenda in establishing the Satyashodak Samaj ('Truth-seeking Society') was to promote a society that was egalitarian when it came to labour, gender, and caste by resisting Brahmin hegemony and abolishing Shudra and Dalit slavery.

Other scholarship on Maharashtra focusses on social reformers in cities like Pune and Bombay: leaders who appeared much closer to their Bengal counterparts, and who were quite conscious of Brahmanical caste conventions, like M. G. Ranade, R. G. Bhandarkar and others. Meera Kosambi (2007) describes the views of someone like Bhandarkar—who sought to placate opponents to women's education by portraying it as a kind of 'patriarchal convergence', such that education was 'a window in the prison house' that would not disturb her place in the home or the discharging of household duties—as a very limited modernising position (Kosambi 2007: 151). This is a more conservative rendering of Partha Chatterjee's 'nationalist resolution of the women's question', whereby social reform was successfully contained by making the educated woman the bearer of Indian tradition in the cultural battle against colonial rule (Chatterjee 1989). Kosambi (2007) brings together the social reform agenda with that of child marriage and enforced widowhood, once again by re-inscribing caste. The education of women had been strongly proscribed under Brahminical norms—it was frequently said that to gain an education was to invite the misfortune of widowhood. Literate women, even daughters of pandits, were seen as potentially subversive, evading household control to engage in immoral relations with non-domestic men. Education in the colonial period, however, lent itself to being contained within an evolving family structure for upwardly mobile, newly educated men who needed literate wives. Kosambi quotes Bal Gangadhar Tilak, the Brahmin conservative and revivalist who, while sharply opposed to the liberal reformers on many issues, including that of child marriage, gave his sanction to a certain form of female education—training to become good wives and mothers, which allowed for primary schooling. She neglects to add that in Tilak's view, primary education was but a beginning—a woman's education is only fulfilled in the marital home, the 'workshop' where she is trained. 'By the age of 15 or 16 years a woman should be well trained at housework and this training will never be available in a school as much as at home. *The marital home is the "workshop" of female education*' (Tilak, cited in Kosambi 2007: 157; emphasis added). Only when such conservative groups were assured that schools would pose no threat to the primary socialisation of the Brahmin family did they participate in promoting a limited form of education for women.

The Rakhmabai Case

What then of the institution of marriage and the question of child marriage? The first major case related to child marriage that sparked a national and international controversy, inviting even the intervention of Queen Victoria herself, was the Rakhmabai case that unfolded in the 1880s. Much has been written about this case and from several perspectives (Chakravarti 2005; Chandra 1998; Heimsath 1964; Kosambi 2007; Masselos 1998). The Rakhmabai case is truly remarkable for several reasons. It pitted the colonial state and its British laws against the complex and multi-layered realm of so-called Hindu law, which encompassed both codified laws and caste-based systems of adjudication. Rakhmabai herself was an unusual example of a woman who, though born into a Shudra family whose traditional occupation was carpentry, had witnessed urbanisation, upward mobility, and the benefits of western education, thanks to a combination of financial security and liberal reformist ideas that characterised her larger familial context in Bombay. Yet, as was customary in those times (possibly also as a mark of taking on Brahminical practices in tandem with rising social status), she had been married in 1875 at the age of eleven to one Dadaji Thakur who, while staying with his maternal uncle, was expected to be groomed by way of education till the time was right for them to live together.

However, this did not happen, and Rakhmabai in subsequent meetings found him incompatible and would not live with him. After various unsuccessful efforts and rather than resort to caste adjudication, in 1884 Dadaji issued a legal notice for restitution of conjugal rights under British law, which was the year that saw the initiation of reform in the realm of child marriage. Rakhmabai refused to yield even when the judgement went against her; the matter went on appeal, with various aspects of Hindu law, British law, and caste practice being drawn upon by the opposing sides, until by 1888 a financial settlement was proposed whereby Dadaji relinquished his rights over her. During the court case, Rakhmabai even took it upon herself to write two letters in English about her condition to the *Times of India*, from which it is worth quoting:

> My English readers can hardly conceive the hard lot entailed upon Hindu women by the custom of early marriage.... The treatment which even servants receive from their European masters is far better than falls to the share of us Hindu women. We are treated worse than beasts.... (cited in Kosambi 2007: 266)

Here was a case in which identifiably feminist protest was articulated, using powerful analogies of feudal oppression and animal cruelty to evoke maximum sympathy. While detractors could only see in Rakhmabai the baneful consequences of westernised education, hers was a case of a bad marriage to an undesirable man with less education and social status compared to her own, yet sanctified both by Hindu and British law. It took until 1891 for the underlying question of child marriage in Hindu law to be subjected to some reform. But that moment belonged to yet another case, one that shook the public world of Calcutta.

The Age of Consent Controversy

This section deals with what can, in retrospect, be described as the processes that made possible the first major legislation concerning child marriage, namely the Age of Consent Bill of 1891 under conditions of colonial rule. This is also a story where, as we shall see, questions of caste reappear only to be folded into notions of Indian culture and tradition, which was enlarged to become a national frame, as distinct from a local or regional one. The story is remarkably complex, bringing in players from different regions of the country. It involved considerable controversy precisely because it pitted those who were prepared to approach the colonial state for matters of social reform, here concerning consent to sexual intercourse (within or outside marriage), against those who believed that nationalist strivings demanded a break from such petitions to the State. This moment has been approached from different perspectives by scholars and continues to be a matter of ongoing debate and investigation.

The Age of Consent Act

By the 1880s, as a consequence of widespread debate, writing, and networking across the sub-continent, reformers in the Bombay Presidency took up in earnest the issue of child marriage. It was not a Hindu but a Parsi—Behramji Malabari—who began the actual process of petitioning the State with his 'Note on Infant Marriage in India' written in 1884, along with another note on enforced widowhood. Note therefore the use of the term 'infant', not even that of 'child'. Traditional upper-caste Hindu marriages could be performed long before puberty (indeed even in infancy) through an alliance between families in which no notion of consent was even conceivable (which could also include the groom). However, such marriages were consummated upon reaching puberty through a second ritual—the *garbhadhan* or impregnation ceremony, after which it was common for the bride to move to the groom's house and begin her new life with all its attendant sexual, reproductive, and household duties as wife and daughter-in-law. The scriptures, it was said, made it clear that menstruation implied the death of the embryo and hence a marriage that took place after puberty would bring dishonour to the ancestors and family lineage. Puberty itself signalled the birth of a woman's sexual desire, which—it was also said—would be out of control if not already contained within the institution of a legitimate marriage. Sexual intercourse and the birth of children (especially sons) were mandatory duties that marriage entailed. These were the descriptions of the institution of Hindu marriage at the heart of the controversy, which reformers were prepared (to a certain degree) to question, but which had to be defended by those in opposition.

Malabari's Note in 1884 referred to infant marriage as a worse evil than infanticide, since it entailed lifelong misery and for both the wife and husband: ill-health and disease, loss of studies for the husband, sickly children, 'a wreck of two lives grown almost old in youth' (cited in Kosambi 2007: 278). These arguments were used by many others in the subsequent campaign, ranging from Jotirao Phule to Pandita Ramabai (in her treatise *The High Caste Hindu Woman*) and also by a small number of the very first feminists of Maharashtra (Anagol 2007). Phule forwarded two Notes of his own, written in English. I find particularly noteworthy (though I have yet to see this discussed in scholarship on Phule) that in his Opinion on Malabari's 'Note on Infant Marriage', Phule openly questioned the false universalism of the 'enlightened Hindu of Bengal', whose suggestions are 'not universal and applicable' to the 'ignorant shudra-atishudras' and 'downtrodden aborigines', amongst whom a young wife could be worked harder 'than an American slave', a bridegroom's family ruined by indebtedness, or conjugal incompatibility due to early marriage end with the girl's suicide (Deshpande 2002: 193–194). While this certainly called for increasing the minimum age of marriage for both boys and girls, it also required change through a non-Brahmin education (ibid.). On the other hand, Phule went on to state, Brahmin women suffer from the degeneracy of the Brahminical institution of marriage, where a man is allowed every excess of polygamy and lust, while after his death, the wife must endure the severest strictures of widowhood, including being forced into prostitution to survive. Either both widows and widowers should not remarry or both be permitted to do so.

Phule thus put forward a differential picture constituted by the intersections of caste, gender, and labour, which was responsible both for the direct victimisation of the Brahmin widow and the state of an uneducated, oppressed Shudr-atishudra people with their own equally disastrous marriage practices. His views should also be seen as a corrective to those who believed that child marriage was only an upper-caste custom. He asked that the girl be at least eleven and the boy nineteen. In spite of his radicalism, this age gap should indicate how differently childhood was perceived, even in Phule's thinking, when it came to boys and girls. Malabari's Note demanded that the age of the girl be raised from ten to twelve years.

Scholars like Tanika Sarkar (2001) and Meera Kosambi (2007) have described at length the enormous opposition this move invited, first in the western region by nationalists like Tilak, and subsequently in Bengal. Opponents to raising the age of consent saw this as a direct affront to shastric injunctions as well as to local caste practices, and castigated reformers for painting a grossly exaggerated picture of the evils of the Hindu custom of infant marriage. Indeed, they went to considerable lengths to describe infant marriage as a marvellous Indian institution, the core of our culture, for which no apologies were required, least of all the intervention of an alien colonial state. These undeniably caste-based sanctions could, however, be redescribed as focusing on ideas of female sexuality that operated as a hinge between norms of culture (in the form of religious sanction) and biology (represented by the female body at its first menarche). Sarkar has demonstrated how the Bengal Presidency was thrown into a frenzy of support for the anti-reformers, for whom the Age of Consent controversy crystallised into the birth of militant nationalism. Large numbers gathered in mass protest in public places, the first of its kind in colonial India. Alternate scriptural views that mentioned higher ages of cohabitation after puberty, newly evolving scientific conceptions of the female body, eugenic notions of breeding a stronger race of children, and moral entreaties were variously drawn upon by those in favour of reform.

According to Sarkar, it was only the Phulmonee case of 1891 that dramatically ended the stalemate. Phulmonee was a young girl, by most accounts married at the age of eleven to a man around thirty years of age; sexual intercourse was so violent that she suffered from severe bleeding, leading to her death (Sarkar 2001). Some contemporary observers have anachronistically called it a fatal case of marital rape. Given that the IPC of 1860 stipulated that the minimum age for sexual intercourse was ten years, the husband was ultimately let off. Change happened at a different level. As Sarkar has gone on to elaborate, the dead body of Phulmonee caused the carefully crafted and aestheticised image of the doll-like infant wife celebrated by Hindu revivalists to collapse. After the Phulmonee case, several other cases involving injury or the death of child brides came to receive more attention, including news reports from different parts of the country.

In 1891, the Age of Consent Bill was passed, which raised the age of consent for sexual activity on the part of a girl, whether within marriage or outside of it, from 10 to 12 years. Geraldine Forbes has commented that this was a compromise, since it did not prevent families from forming a marriage alliance at an earlier age, and then waiting for its consummation when the girl was 12 (Forbes 1979: 410). Further, Himani Bannerji (2001), in her careful analysis of the judgement, has observed that 'consent' here actually had little to do with notions of a girl's right to choose, and was instead about the right of legal guardians to alienate a woman's body to a man, whether as husband or client.

The details of the Phulmonee case and the battles surrounding the passing of the Age of Consent Bill would imply that it is quite unclear what place, if any, can be accorded to notions of consent understood as women's agency in the passing of this Act. I would like to suggest that the Age of Consent Bill achieved something else. It should be seen as the first critical moment in the invention of girlhood in India, in which the question of caste, which was so central in western India, could be subsumed within a battle over national culture.

Concluding Questions

In the above account, I have tried to deconstruct the ways in which caste appears and disappears in existing histories of social reform. A figure like Phule brought to life a different language of social justice, and viewed caste as a kind of double structure, one with disastrous consequences for both Brahmin and Shudra/Atishudra women. Phule's legacy, unfortunately, was largely lost after his death. Influential accounts of 'women' in the battle over national culture at the turn of the nineteenth century do not refer to this strand of political and social struggle. It required the twentieth-century leader Babasaheb Ambedkar to revisit Phule's binary view of caste and introduce a new frame, that of graded inequalities. It is surely noteworthy that Ambedkar's battles over untouchability and the annihilation of caste were equally and critically all about gender. Here too, while critical engagements with his life and work are certainly underway, the field of women's studies has yet to be substantially benefitted.

Today the questions of Indian culture and of women's position within it are locked together even more tenaciously and violently under the conditions of majoritarian Hindutva politics. The women's studies classroom is more differentiated than ever before, thanks in large part to the implementation of reservations. Unfortunately, we as teachers have largely failed in turning such a heterogeneous classroom into an opportunity. What is worse, we often collude in perpetuating caste and class divides, whether by omission or commission. At the same time, it is also my argument that we inherit a longer history of the problematic presence/absence of caste in understanding gender. In this chapter I have suggested revisiting this history where, thanks to newer scholarship, we can perhaps better recognise how we might tell this very history differently. This may be one strategy to bring caste and its elusive presence into our pedagogic practices.

References

Anagol, Padma. 2007. 'Rebellious Wives and Dysfunctional Marriages: Indian Women's Discourses and Participation in the Debates over Restitution of Conjugal Rights and the Child Marriage Controversy in the 1880s and 1890s'. In *Women and Social Reform in Modern India*, Tanika Sarkar and Sumit Sarkar (eds): 420–465. Ranikhet: Permanent Black.

Bannerji, Himani. 2001. *Inventing Subjects: Studies in Hegemony, Patriarchy and Colonialism*. New Delhi: Tulika Press.

Carroll, Lucy. 2007. 'Law, Custom and Statutory Social Reform: The Hindu Widows' Remarriage Act of 1856'. In *Women and Social Reform in Modern India, Volume 1*, Tanika Sarkar and Sumit Sarkar (eds): 113–144. Ranikhet: Permanent Black.

Chakravarti, Uma. 2005. *The Life and Times of Pandita Ramabai*. New Delhi: Zubaan Books.

Chandra, Sudhir. 1998. *Enslaved Daughters: Colonialism, Law and Women's Rights*. Delhi: Oxford University Press.

Chatterjee, Partha. 1989. 'The Nationalist Resolution of the Women's Question'. In *Recasting Women: Essays in Colonial History*, Kumkum Sangari and Sudesh Vaid (eds): 233–253. New Delhi: Kali for Women.

______. 1993. *The Nation and its Fragments: Colonial and Postcolonial Histories*. Princeton, NJ: Princeton University Press.

Chowdhry, Prem. 1993. 'Conjugality, Law and State: Inheritance Rights as Pivot of Control in Northern India'. *National Law School Journal, Special Issue on Feminism and Law* 1: 95–115.

Deshpande, Govind P. 2002. *Selected Writings of Jotirao Phule*. New Delhi: Leftword Books.

Forbes, Geraldine H. 1979. 'Women and Modernity: The Issue of Child Marriage in India'. *Women's Studies International Quarterly* 2: 407–419.

______. 1986. 'In Search of the Pure Heathen: Missionary Women in Nineteenth Century India'. *Economic and Political Weekly* 21 (17): WS2–WS8.

______. 1998. *Women in Modern India*. Cambridge: Cambridge University Press.

Heimsath, C. H. 1964. *Indian Nationalism and Hindu Social Reform*. Princeton University Press.

Kosambi, Meera. 2007. *Crossing Thresholds: Feminist Essays in Social History*. New Delhi and Ranikhet: Permanent Black.

Mani, Lata. 1989. 'Contentious Traditions: The Debate on Sati in Colonial India'. In *Recasting Women: Essays in Colonial History*, Kumkum Sangari and Sudesh Vaid (eds): 88–126. New Delhi: Kali for Women.

Masselos, Jim. 1998. 'Sexual Property/Sexual Violence: Wives in Late Nineteenth Century Bombay'. In *Images of Women in Maharashtrian Society*, Anne Feldhaus (ed.): 113–134. New York: State University of New York Press.

Nair, Janaki. 1994. *Women and the Law in Colonial India: A Social History*. New Delhi: Kali for Women.

O'Hanlon, Rosalind. 1994. *A Comparison between Women and Men: Tarabai Shinde and the Critique of Gender Relations in Colonial India*. Chennai: Oxford University Press.

______. 2014. *At the Edges of Empire: Essays in the Social and Intellectual History of India*. Ranikhet: Permanent Black.

Rege, Sharmila (ed.). 2006. *Writing Caste, Writing Gender: Narrating Dalit Women's Testimonios*. New Delhi: Zubaan.

______. 2008. 'Introduction to *Writing Caste, Writing Gender: Dalit Women's Testimonios*'. In *Women's Studies in India: A Reader*, Mary E. John (ed.): 452–458. New Delhi: Penguin.

Sarkar, Sumit, and Tanika Sarkar (eds). 2007. *Women and Social Reform in Modern India, Volumes 1 and 2*. Ranikhet: Permanent Black.

Sarkar, Tanika. 2001. *Hindu Wife, Hindu Nation: Community, Religion, and Cultural Nationalism*. Bloomington: Indiana University Press.

Seth, Sanjay. 2007. *Subject Lessons: The Western Education of Colonial India*. Durham: Duke University Press.

Sharma, Kumud, and C. P. Sujaya (eds). 2012. *Towards Equality: Report of the Committee on the Status of Women in India* (reprint with a new introduction). New Delhi: Pearson Education.

Sinha, Mrinalini. 1994. *Colonial Masculinities: The Manly Englishman and Effeminate Bengali*. Manchester: Manchester University Press.

Part II

Women's Studies and its Institutionalisation

3

Teaching Resistance and Critique

Some Reflections on Women's Studies in an Interdisciplinary Institution

U. Vindhya

Women's studies in India can be said to have 'a long past, but only a short history'. This statement by Hermann Ebbinghaus (1908), referring to the discipline of psychology in the West, is perhaps applicable to women's studies as well, indicating its short history as a formally defined field, but a fairly long past of the 'women's question' in public consciousness. Therefore, while concerns related to oppression and discrimination of women have been voiced for over one and a half centuries, associated with the period of social reform in India, the birth, so to speak, of women's studies—with an explicit focus on the marginalisation of women in society and within systems of knowledge production, and the formal inclusion of such a discipline in higher education in India—is just about a quarter of a century old.

The nature of the discipline of women's studies has always been one of ongoing negotiation with the biases in existing systems of knowledge production and in all aspects of social life—family, economy, culture, State—which are brought under critical scrutiny. While this critique has resulted in a burgeoning literature and significant policy changes over the past few decades, critical engagement with higher education in particular has not been the focus of much review. Although the institutional presence of women's studies in higher education is apparent by now, its expected function as a facilitator for social change through its academic programmes has not received as much critical attention. What is also lesser known and discussed is the classroom experience of how and what of this body of knowledge is being communicated to the students; what are the challenges in pedagogy, and the sites of resistance within the institution. Concern over whether women's studies as an academic programme is being able to play an interventionary/transformatory role in higher education in accordance with its original mandate when it was introduced in the 1980s is the prime motivator for this chapter.

While inaugurating the first conference of the newly-formed Indian Association for Women's Studies (IAWS) in 1981, Madhuri Shah, then chairperson of the University Grants Commission (UGC), observed that the introduction of separate women's studies programmes was a 'temptation' (cited in John 2008: 5), hinting at the highly contentious question of whether women's studies should be seen as an autonomous discipline or as a critical perspective integrated into all disciplines. Be that as it may, and despite the prevailing perception at the time that any move to introduce it as a separate discipline should be opposed, we have witnessed the introduction of Master's/MPhil./PhD courses in women's studies in several universities since the late 1980s–1990s. Mostly anchored by Women's Studies Centres (WSCs) in the universities, which were established by the initiative of the UGC, these courses were introduced also in the wake of a pioneering research programme sponsored by the Indian Council of Social Science Research (ICSSR) in the late 1970s.

Furthermore, reflecting the need for 'new knowledge about women' (John 2008), there has been a veritable explosion of literature over the past three decades or so, primarily undertaken by self-identified women's studies scholars allied to and anchored in other disciplines. This burgeoning literature is reflected in an increasing number of books brought out by publishing houses, the growing community of scholars interested in conducting research in the area, and the inclusion of the 'gender perspective/women's issues' in courses across the social science and humanities, indicating its deeper incorporation into other disciplines. For instance, the ICSSR-commissioned decadal reviews of research in sociology and psychology now include research from these disciplines that are imbued with a gender perspective (Bharat 2001; Chouhan 2009; Vindhya 2011). These reviews have also included research published in journals and edited volumes that are outside the disciplinary boundaries of sociology and psychology, signalling that the search for topics related to gender often extends beyond such demarcated lines. Similarly, women's studies scholars from different social science disciplines have interrogated the knowledge and curricula of their home disciplines through the critical lens provided by women's studies, some notable examples being economics (Dewan 1999), history (Chakravarti 2006), and sociology (Rege 2003).

It appears then that women's studies has come of age, with a substantial corpus of knowledge generated and available for designing and introducing courses in higher education, resulting in the expansion of the base and boundaries of the field. The critique of existing biases in systems of knowledge production and of all aspects of social life—family, economy, culture, and State—has remained at the heart of the discipline, and has resulted in a burgeoning literature and significant policy changes over the past few decades. However, education, particularly higher education, as a site of radical change has not been the focus of as much review and critical engagement. There have of course been the occasional seminars, for instance a Centre for Women's Development Studies seminar titled 'Engendering Disciplines, Disciplining Gender' (John 2008) and sub-theme/panel discussions held during the IAWS conferences (1981–2017) signalling the institutional presence, albeit limited, of women's studies in higher education. However, its expected function as a facilitator for social change through its academic programmes (Krishnaraj 2012) has not received as much critical attention. While the vast inter- and multi-disciplinary research literature has amply demonstrated the multiple inequalities between the genders, the classroom experience of *how* and *what* of this body of knowledge is being communicated to students has not received enough attention. Some exceptional examples include attempts like that of Rehana Ghadially (1994) who analyses the experience of teaching women's studies to engineering students and a more recent study by S. Nagalia (2018) on the challenges of designing and teaching gender studies in a newly established social science and humanities university. In all this, the question remains of whether the inclusion of women's studies has been able to revitalise higher education by generating new knowledge and bringing social issues closer to practice, which in turn is expected to bring a change in attitudes, counter reactionary forces, and signal greater participation and inclusion of women in the higher education system. Moreover, another aspect that remains under-studied despite its implications for the socialisation process of education—that is, its 'hidden curriculum', to borrow a phrase from Philip Jackson (1968) and B. Snyder (1970)—is the set of challenges in pedagogy, and the sites of resistance within the classroom.

Contextualising this concern about the interventionary/transformatory role of women's studies within a premier social sciences university such as Tata Institute of Social Sciences (TISS), this chapter draws on faculty experiences of teaching women's studies—including misgivings and apprehensions, as well as our small triumphs and pleasures—in the early years (2012–2017) of its inception in the Hyderabad campus. The chapter focuses on two key themes: (*a*) the implications of the location of a transdisciplinary subject such as women's studies in an interdisciplinary educational institution; and (*b*) the practice of feminist pedagogy and reflections on power relations in the classroom.

Transdisciplinary Women's Studies in an Interdisciplinary Institution

Beginning its journey as the first institution in South Asia in 1936 dedicated to social work education and to producing professionals in the field, TISS is currently unique for its array of interdisciplinary Master's and doctoral programmes across multiple campuses and has expanded phenomenally from the primary focus on social work at the time of its inception.

TISS Hyderabad was established in 2012 as one of the off-campuses of the institution, on the invitation of the government of undivided Andhra Pradesh. Set up primarily as a response to the over-emphasis on technology training, at the expense of social science education in the state in particular and in southern India in general, the establishment of the campus was preceded by several scoping studies and national consultative meetings. It was in this context and in light of the perceived status of social science education that the conceptualisation and designing of curricula was expected to be, as the initial vision document states,

> in tune with the critical challenges confronting contemporary societies [and] to train and equip students... with perspectives, knowledge, skills and abilities to comprehend historical, social, political and economic processes from the standpoints of various social sciences, and to intervene in important social issues that shape people's lives. (Proposal for Integrated Master's Programme 2012)

The keywords in the vision document were therefore to provide students with the perspectives and skills necessary for *understanding*, *analysis*, and *intervention* in the processes and dynamics of social change. Courses were hence designed with this mandate and aimed to create a balanced emphasis on theory and experiential learning and on the integration of social science knowledge rather than creating vertical and exclusive silos of expertise.

It was in line with this initial vision that the Integrated MPhil.–PhD programme in women's studies was introduced within the very first year of the establishment of the off-campus in 2012, followed by the Master's programme in 2014. Women's studies was no stranger to the institution, having been started in the parent campus of Mumbai way back in 1982.[1] But importantly, the ease with which the programme was set up in TISS Hyderabad was indicative of the nature of TISS itself—an institution wherein the authority of conventional subjects of study was not absolute, and where theoretical and methodological pluralism as well as interdisciplinary and crossdisciplinary academic work was encouraged and made to flourish.

The nature and status of women's studies as an interdisciplinary programme thus seemed to fit in with other programmes that were products of interdisciplinarity, propelled by 'the new species of integration, collaboration, complexity, critique, and problem solving' (Klein 2009: 15). Following Natalie Porter and others, if we define *discipline* as 'having a central problem with items considered to be facts relevant to that problem, and having explanations, goals, and theories related to the problem' (cited in Wagner, et al. 2011: 15), the 'central problem' in women's studies is the dynamics of oppression and power. It is here that the discipline diverged somewhat from the other programmes. The foundations of women's studies lay in drawing from a broad range of disciplinary approaches to the study of women and gender, with an underlying thematic focus on the complexities of power and asymmetries in gender relations. The same cannot be said to be the case with the other programmes which do not have such a distinctive focus on power imbalances.

In keeping with the trend towards interdisciplinary research witnessed since the 1970s, signifying a shift towards a 'problem orientation' (Schmidt 2008), the focus on an instrumental function of problem orientation marked the field of women's studies as interdisciplinary. Indeed, exponents of interdisciplinary research note that an emphasis on application orientation and problem-solving is a key reason for the emergence of interdisciplinary research (Wagner, et al. 2011). Drawing on these conceptualisations, one may argue that the establishment of women's studies in an institution such as TISS was not facilitated only by the initial support received from the UGC in the form of funding. Rather, the status of women's studies as an interdisciplinary course was perceived to be in consonance with the vision of the institution to produce socially sensitive human service professionals dedicated to the core values of social justice and promotion of sustainable development, and committed to move beyond academics and focus on social problem-solving.

In my view, what further facilitated the easy assimilation of women's studies into the interdisciplinary programmes across TISS is this emphasis on *professional preparation with a vocational focus*, identified as a key category in the typology of interdisciplinary fields suggested by Raymond Miller (1982). Indeed, professional preparation and the heightened mandate of problem-solving is cited as a major ingredient for the emergence of fields such as social work, management studies, media studies, public policy and planning, and so on.

Here too, a key difference between other programmes of study and women's studies lies, however, in the manner in which the former is distinguished by the 'integrating, interacting and linking' features of interdisciplinarity (Klein 2009) while women's studies is characterised by 'transcending, transgressing and transforming' features of transdisciplinarity. While the mandate of *application, problem-solving* and *professional preparation* is readily accepted and fit in well within the overarching mission of the institution, it is the *transgressing and transforming* role that often creates a sense of unease.

By way of illustration, I would like to cite a few observations made by students enrolled in a course on philosophy and methods of social research, a foundational course with a combined classroom for students of all the Master's programmes (around 150 students). I was teaching a module on the influence of feminist perspectives on social science research and began the class by asking the students to think of any example to illustrate the relevance of the categories of women and gender to social science research and why we should learn about feminist influences on social science research. To begin with, students of both the rural development and public policy programmes cited examples of sati and such others to demonstrate the historical disadvantage experienced by women, but they did not mention contemporary concerns like unequal access to resources and the disproportionate burden of domestic responsibilities on women and girls. This made me wonder, drawing from Judith Lorber (1994), whether it is easier for students to relate to gender as a process of social construction that creates the differences that define men and women, rather than as a system of social stratification ranking men above women of the same class and other social markers, or as an institution that structures all aspects of life including work, family, sexuality, and emotional life.

However, even this understanding of gender seemed to be coloured by the historical legacy of restricting women to the private sphere, which was sometimes accepted by students and justified by appeals to protection of women as a class on moral and physical grounds, viewing motherhood as a woman's central place, and subscribing to essentialist notions of parenting. For instance, in a discussion on stereotypes and the need to deconstruct/dismantle them, several students of other programmes spoke of the priceless value of '*ma ka banaya hua khana*' (food cooked and served with love by mother, as the phrase implies) and of woman/mother as the prime nurturer and questioned what was wrong with the scheme of male protector/provider and female nurturer since both are equally necessary roles. When I pointed out the inherent problem in this 'separate but equal' construction of gender roles, some of them insisted that with increasing emphasis on equality and equal access to resources such as education, girls these days were in any case transgressing traditional roles. I realised that it was more difficult perhaps for students of other disciplines to scrutinise and challenge their own assumptions and beliefs about gender, but relatively easier and less cognitively dissonant for them to critically analyse government programmes, and to come up with policy briefs on the inclusion of gender in these programmes as part of their curricular learning.

This realisation was further bolstered when I was explaining the challenge that feminist research poses to sexist and androcentric erasures and bias in conventional research and that feminism engages critically with the nature of knowledge, society, and power. A few students murmured that this seems to be '*not Tata Institute of Social Sciences, but Tata Institute of Feminist Sciences*'—an observation perhaps fuelled by the fact that the key administrative and decision-making positions in the Institute at that point of time were held by women faculty. It also brings into sharp relief the continuing challenge to gender equality: there are enduring contradictions between a democratic political system with its constitutional guarantees of equality and a hierarchical social system that has scant regard for these guarantees. How then does one deal with equality in everyday interpersonal interactions and relationships? This remains a crucial challenge and an obstacle for social change, the avowed goal of women's studies.

While the inclusion of women's studies in higher education does seem to have led to the placing of 'women' in the content lists of the academy, and brought everyday reality into the academy, discussions on stereotypes and their multiform enduring patriarchal manifestations continue to be met with resistance and skepticism within and outside the classroom. Students of other programmes have reportedly said that it is their courses which deal with 'tough real-life problems' whereas women's studies is 'airy-fairy' and preoccupied with 'individualist' issues such as sexuality. Students seem to be relatively ready to engage with macro structures of disadvantage and inequality such as caste and class; however, challenging the category of gender and its intersectionalities with other social structures, beginning with their own personal lives, appears to be more intimidating given it requires reflecting on intimate spaces of everyday life and personal relationships. The perspective of intersectionality of caste, class, *and* gender disadvantage, which is included in the academic curriculum, thus seems to be limited to theoretical acceptance.

The purported association of women's studies with sexuality and sexual freedom resonates with students of women's studies as well. In the present times, these new messages that convey possibilities of freedom of choice, autonomy, and personal identity seem to especially captivate privileged students (both men and women) seeking admission to this course of study. The original context of the emergence of women's studies, rooted in the demonstration and documentation of multiple inequalities between (mostly) men and women and the critique of dominant disciplinary approaches to knowledge production, appears in their view to be stale, and seems to have given way at present to these new perceptions of gender.

While students seeking admission to women's studies seem to be attracted to and animated by the goal of personal transformation and change, the objective of social change is couched in the 'do-good impulse' to change the lives of 'long-suffering women in the villages'. While the intention may be laudable to begin with, as an indicator of their social responsiveness, social change is perceived to be 'doing good' for others more disadvantaged than them, and there is an expectation that the knowledge gained will eventually prepare them for careers in the development sector.

The nomenclature of 'women's studies' has also invited a great deal of critical commentary by students from other disciplines as well as from women's studies. While students seemed to approve the name of the School, 'Gender Studies', indicating its purported broader reach for male and transgender students, the name of the programme itself, 'Women's Studies', was interpreted either as narrow and outdated by some or as a political choice by others. A related remark on the inclusion of courses such as 'Men and Masculinities' in the programme was that it was indicative of an attempt made by the discipline to be more 'inclusive', in contrast to its earlier focus on the overrepresentation of women as victims. Such courses were also perceived as being in line with the growing interest, particularly in the development sector, in working with men and on understanding hegemonic masculinities as an obstacle for social change.

Further, the emphasis on problem-solving and vocational preparation leads to a key contradiction. The dissonance lies in the need for critical discussion and production of ideas to generate alternative knowledge production and foster social change on the one hand, and processing of graduates for career-readiness on the other. This came into sharp relief during our campus placement, when potential employers apparently remarked that the women's studies students 'were strong on theory' but not so on 'application and state programmes and policies for women'. This led to considerable discussions in school meetings on whether our courses were excessively theory-laden. One concrete spin-off of these discussions was a series of workshops titled 'Gender and Public Policy', by invited faculty including academics and practitioners, to provide students with critical understanding of state policies and programmes related to women and gender in key areas such as health, education, and livelihood; the historical evolution and shifts in these policies; and their current impact. While these thematic areas had been included as an integral part of the courses, a concerted focus on how state policies have evolved and their current status now aimed to enhance students' career-readiness, particularly in the development sector. Another effort to strengthen the acceptability of women's studies as a career choice was to include in a national conference in March 2015 a panel discussion titled 'Beckoning Futures', featuring representatives from the government, development sector, publishing industry, and academia to spell out what the future holds in terms of careers and growth opportunities for women's studies students.

One experience related to student placements reflects the widespread perception that women's studies is only about critique (and hence by implication negative and not constructive). There was an oft-heard remark made by some recruiters: they reportedly asked our students whether they would engage in '*dharnabazi*' (protest culture) and such other 'obstructionist' tactics. With our students often in competition with students from other programmes and vying for jobs from the same placement pie, the instrumental function of women's studies as a career choice has always been a concern for the faculty, since they do not want to be perceived as pushing through an academic programme that did not yield easily to jobs. However, despite attempts by the School to mould its curricula content for career-readiness, and the fact that it has secured amongst the highest number of student placements, any success in placements is often attributed to the relatively privileged 'English-speaking metropolitan' background of our students, whose exterior confidence and presentation skills are seen to be the deciding factors rather than the relevance of the discipline itself for bringing about social change.

Given the large number of governmental and non-governmental organisations in the development sector which have an increasing demand for gender specialists and professionals, the acceptability of women's studies and 'tolerance' to the discipline (despite concerns of funding in an under-funded public institution) thus stems from market factors and its perceived income potential.

Infusing Feminist Pedagogy in the Classroom

Feminist teaching is not just 'good teaching'. Integral to the principles and strategies of pedagogy in the women's studies classroom is the issue of values and attitudes. Although I have been a professional teacher for two decades, it was only when I began to teach courses in this programme that this struck me as a central idea that is essential for the vitality and relevance of women's studies to students. While the delivery of content is obviously a key aim, an underlying but enduring principle is the commitment to a feminist process in the classroom. We did not apply a feminist process of teaching at the outset (nor did we have any developed guidelines in this regard) but through conversations amongst faculty, either informally or in formal faculty meetings at the school level, what emerged for me was a broad template of feminist-inspired principles and teaching practices. While reflections and alertness to power relations between the researcher and the researched now form an integral component of methodology and research ethics courses (primarily at the MPhil./doctoral levels), what was more subtle and indirect was the consciousness of how a teacher conducts herself in terms of power relations in student–teacher/supervisor interactions.

Drawing from the principles developed by Natalie Porter and Melba Vasquez (1997) to guide feminist supervision for counselling practice, I configured the following philosophy to be useful for my own interactions:

Vigilance about Abuses of Power in and Outside the Classroom

Given the hierarchal structures of our educational institutions, which in turn reflect social hierarchies beyond the academy, the principle of vigilance about abuses of power is one that needs constant and keen attention. Teaching women's studies is an experience that weaves into its pedagogy the need to be proactive in analysing power dynamics and differentials between teacher/supervisor and students. The notion of 'power over (others)' in the feminist typology of power (Rowlands 1997) seemed such an easy mantle to slip into rather than the more empowering 'power with' or 'power to' which may initiate and bring about change. However, the former ('power over') is a constant reminder to be alert about one's own conduct in order to democratise relations in institutional spaces while the latter ('power to') serves as a broader aspirational goal for social change.

Collaborative Model of Interpersonal Relationships

Closely related to the need to guard against possible abuses of power is the effort to base interpersonal relationships between teachers and students and amongst faculty on a collaborative and mutually respectful model. The relationships between teachers and students are particularly tricky given the inherently hierarchical nature of this dynamic, which is often perceived to be incompatible with the stated aim of the institution to encourage students' autonomy and diverse perspectives. While insistence on adherence to institutional norms and regulations was generally not perceived as a display of power and authority, given the internalisation of long years of deference to the institutional power of teachers in school, what was seen as imposition of power was the ideological supremacy of the teacher's point of view. As several incidents, both in the women's studies classroom and in other courses revealed, this required carefully balanced and often contentious negotiation with having to communicate 'secular, progressive, social justice values of feminism(s)' while simultaneously listening to students' perspectives that were often at variance with these ideas and which could be labelled as casteist and sexist.

Reflexive Interactions based on Openness, Authenticity, Lifelong Learning, and Self-examination

Encapsulating the feminist slogan of 'personal is political', many of our women's studies faculty shared personal anecdotes about experiences of discrimination and stereotyping, and negotiating work-life balance (especially with caregiving responsibilities of young children and/or the elderly) that helped them redefine personal struggles as did social/political problems shared by many women. Doing so allowed us to appreciate the linkages between personal experiences and societal structures. The emphasis on *life experience* is indeed not only a reflection of the 'personal is political' slogan but is also tied to the formation and restructuring of new interdisciplinary domains. For example, the typology of interdisciplinary fields suggested by Miller (1982) identified life experience as a pertinent category of interdisciplinarity with the emergence of women's studies and ethnic studies (Dalit studies and tribal studies may be seen as similar examples in India). Amongst students in particular, my own observation is that it is this life experience, a sense of personal transformation, of personal identity formation and assertion, and, of making political choices regarding sexual orientation, of choices related to career and marriage, and in general of choices related to the kind of life they wish to live—reflections that women's studies curriculum and pedagogy encourage—that has come to represent new perceptions of gender in recent times. However, how one can combine and simultaneously pursue the twin goals of personal and social transformation and change is an ongoing challenge.

Finally, drawing from Ellen Kimmel and Judith Worell (1997) I conclude by highlighting what in my view are key dimensions—risks, challenges, and rewards—of the personal experience of being a feminist teacher. Risks include backlash to feminism, stigmatisation and devaluing of feminist scholarship, and overextension from too many demands on time and energy. As mentioned earlier, our students discussed a common perception amongst other students that while their courses reflected 'real world' problems and consequently elicited tough and rigorous scholarship and application, women's studies seemed to indicate soft scholarship, owing perhaps to its emphasis on the ontological nature of the discipline. Such a distinction is indicative perhaps of the continued presence of the Cartesian hierarchical dualism of man/intellect/culture and woman/emotion/nature. Challenges include struggling with appropriate use of power with peers and students, becoming a realistic and useful role model for students, attending to the impact of feminist teaching on students' academic and personal lives, and assessing the effects of feminist pedagogy on the individual, institution, and the larger social system. However, the rewards are gratifying, in the sense that there is congruence between personal values and professional life, participation in students' personal growth and empowerment, and a sense of meaning and purpose associated with participation in social change either in the form of writing, gender-sensitisation training, and/or other forms of activism. In addition to endowing a sense of purpose, the infusion of feminist pedagogy provides visibility and voice to women's studies students in the institution and academic community, while signalling to faculty, staff, and students the enduring 'political' nature of the 'personal'.

Wrapping Up

The purpose of introducing women's studies in the higher education system, according to its pioneers, was to conscientise students to the position of women in the dynamic of individual and social action and life; to play an interventionary role in higher education; and to be a catalyst for social change (Krishnaraj 2012). In short, the discipline was to play a transformative role, introducing a new perspective into intellectual and academic life, a significant part of this perspective being the focus on the gendered subject in the social sciences and the recognition that 'the once universal he/man of academic disciplines is only one half of human existence' (Evans 1997: 25). Along with the primary goal of reconstructing knowledge was the equally fundamental aim of reconstructing the social world by identifying patriarchy and its intersections with other forms of social hegemony that produce and perpetuate inequalities, and by interrogating the order of relations between men and women (and amongst other genders as well).

However, universities and public-funded institutions in particular no longer occupy the same space, status, or autonomy as they did in previous decades. The location of women's studies within this contemporary context is compromised by the character of an under-funded institution attempting to implement public expectations of higher education on a large scale with little additional funding. We are living in times when funding issues determine the sustainability of academic programmes, when the 'processing' of graduate students for employability seems to be of paramount importance, rather than the discussion and production of ideas, which was the original link between the women's movement and higher education institutions. When the increased tolerance to women's studies seems to stem more from its potential to churn out 'young professionals' who can oversee and execute state programmes related to women's empowerment, the 'processing of graduates' takes precedence over critical understanding of systems of exclusion, discrimination, and oppression.

Note

1. The Centre for Women's Studies was established with UGC support in the parent campus in Mumbai in 1982 and was subsequently upgraded to an Advanced Centre in 2011. Continued and sustained UGC funding to the Centre has now become questionable, with the future of not only the TISS centre but of several such centres across the country hanging in a precarious balance.

References

Bharat, Shalini. 2001. 'On the Periphery: Psychology of Gender'. In *Psychology in India Revisited: Developments in the Discipline, vol. 2, Personality and Health Psychology*, Janak Pandey (ed.): 300–355. New Delhi: Sage.

Chakravarti, Uma. 2006. *History as Practice, in Everyday Lives, Everyday Histories: Beyond the Kings and Brahmans of 'Ancient' India*. New Delhi: Tulika Books.

Chouhan, Neeta. 2009. 'Women's Studies'. In *Sociology and Social Anthropology in India,* Yogesh Atal (ed.): 302–358. New Delhi: Pearson Education.

Dewan, Ritu. 1999. 'Gender in Neo-classical Economics: A Conceptual Overview'. In *From Myths to Markets: Essays on Gender*, Kumkum Sangari and Uma Chakravarti (eds): 312–320. New Delhi: Manohar Publishers.

Ebbinghaus, H. 1908. *Psychology: An Elementary Textbook*. New York: Arno Press.

Evans, Mary. 1997. *Introducing Contemporary Feminist Thought*. Cambridge: Polity Press.

Ghadially, Rehana. 1994. 'Teaching Women's Studies to Male Engineers: A Personal Account'. *Economic & Political Weekly* 29 (3): 753–759.

Jackson, Philip. 1968. *Life in Classrooms.* New York: Teachers' College Press.

John, Mary. 2008. 'Introduction'. In *Women's Studies: A Reader*: 1–18. New Delhi: Penguin Books.

Kimmel, Ellen, and Judith Worell. 1997. 'Preaching What We Practice: Principles and Strategies of Feminist Pedagogy'. In *Shaping the Future of*

Feminist Psychology: Education, Research and Practice, Judith Worell and Norine Johnson (eds): 121–153. Washington DC: American Psychological Association.

Klein, Julie Thompson. 2009. 'Typologies of Interdisciplinarity: The Boundary Work of Definition'. In *The Oxford Handbook of Interdisciplinarity,* Robert Frodeman, Julie T. Klein, and Roberto Pacheco (eds): 15–30. Oxford: Oxford University Press.

Krishnaraj, Maitreyi. 2012. 'Women's Studies in Academia and Development Discourse'. The 22nd J.P. Naik Memorial Lecture Series, 27 September, India International Centre, New Delhi.

Lorber, Judith. 1994. *Paradoxes of Gender.* Yale: Yale University Press.

Miller, Raymond. 1982. 'Varieties of Interdisciplinary Approaches in the Social Sciences'. *Issues in Integrative Studies* 1: 1–37.

Nagalia, S. 2018. 'Conceptualizing Gender Studies: Curriculum and Pedagogy'. *Indian Journal of Gender Studies* 25 (1): 79–107.

Porter, Natalie, and Melba Vasquez. 1997. 'Covision: Feminist Supervision, Process and Collaboration'. In *Shaping the Future of Feminist Psychology: Education, Research and Practice,* Judith Worell and Norine Johnson (eds): 155–171. Washington DC: American Psychological Association.

Proposal for Integrated Master's Programme in Social Sciences. 2012. TISS Hyderabad, January.

Rege, Sharmila. 2003. *Sociology of Gender: The Challenge of Feminist Sociological Knowledge.* New Delhi: Sage.

Rowlands, Jo. 1997. *Questioning Empowerment: Working with Women in Honduras.* Oxford: Oxfam.

Schmidt, John. 2008. 'Towards a Philosophy of Interdisciplinarity'. *Poiesis & Praxis* 5 (1): 53–69.

Snyder, B. 1970. *The Hidden Curriculum.* Boston: MIT Press.

Vindhya, Undurti. 2011. 'Issues of Gender in Psychology: Traversing from Sex Differences to Quality of Women's Lives'. In *Psychology in India, vol. 4: Theoretical and Methodological Developments,* Girishwar Misra (ed.): 145–164. New Delhi: Pearson.

Wagner, Caroline, David Roessner, Kamau Bobb, Julie Klein, Kevin Boyack, Joann Keyton, Ismael Rafols, and Katy Borner. 2011. 'Approaches to Understanding and Measuring Interdisciplinary Scientific Research (IDR): A Review of the Literature'. *Journal of Informetrics* 5(1): 14–26.

4 Interdisciplinarity and Women's Studies Degrees
Some Questions

Arpita Anand

Introduction

The emergence of women's studies as an academic field in India is rife with contradictions: it was envisioned as an intervention within systems where it was yet to enter and establish a space for itself. In higher education, women's studies was assigned the task of 'revitalis[ing] university education, bringing it closer to burning social issues' (University of Delhi 1985: 3); within teaching and research, it was conceptualised as an interdisciplinary, critical perspective that would intervene in all disciplines but would not become a discipline in its own right (SNDT Women's University 1981). This consistent emphasis on '*not* becoming a discipline' suggests that any notion of interdisciplinarity presupposes—and has been understood against and limited by—the idea of a *discipline*. This is equally true of women's studies in other contexts as well, where interdisciplinarity is posed as a question of whether or not women's studies ought to be a discipline (see Allen and Kitch 1998; Friedman 1998 for debates in the American context).

The emergence of women's studies degrees is marked by the unprecedented expansion in higher education in the Eleventh Plan (2007–2012) and the Twelfth Plan (2012–2017) periods. As scholars have noted, equally unprecedented is the much greater focus on the public university in these plans (John 2011). Further, the corresponding University Grants Commission Guidelines for

Women's Studies for these Plan periods urge Women's Studies Centres (WSCs) to offer degrees and move towards becoming departments, thereby shifting the focus more onto women's studies as a teaching field even in official guidelines (Rege 2011). Coming to the questions structuring this chapter, prominent committees on higher education over the past decade have emphasised interdisciplinarity as a feature of what is understood as an 'international' model of universities.[1] In this period, when the market and state policy both are pushing for interdisciplinarity as desirable to more integrated models of knowledge and greater innovation, this chapter will highlight the contradictory experiences of women's studies vis-à-vis the idea of interdisciplinarity. In other words, it is not so much to define or understand what interdisciplinary means or how it is executed in women's studies but rather an exploration of what this persistent claim to interdisciplinarity means for women's studies degrees.

The immediate context also requires some thought as it has bearings on the shape these questions have acquired. As the UGC-sponsored WSCs form the predominant institutional location for women's studies degrees, the present uncertainty around their funding and future existence has rendered the future of the field unpredictable. The primary fieldwork for the project from which this chapter is drawn was undertaken during 2016–2017 and four of the chosen sites are directly caught up in this uncertainty. The sense of marginality of women's studies has resurfaced—not that it was ever entirely absent. Yet the push for women's studies as a teaching field had much to do with legitimisation; degrees and the emphasis on rigour have been central to countering academic marginalisation. So the dilemmas around interdisciplinarity in its relation to disciplinary status and legitimacy acquired a new urgency in this moment of crisis.

This chapter discusses the questions of interdisciplinarity in women's studies with reference to degree programmes offered over the past decade based on the experience of five institutional locations offering such degrees. As part of a larger project,[2] the MA and research degrees in women's studies[3] were studied at five universities across two regions of India: a state university (University A), a public 'professional' university (University B), a central university that is a minority institution (University C), a central university in a metropolitan city (University D), and a state university dedicated to the social sciences (University E).[4]

The first section will discuss the broader meanings of interdisciplinarity for women's studies as a field. The second section draws on specific questions about theory and pedagogy raised from the chosen institutional locations to reflect on how the framework of 'lack of boundaries' is central to the interdisciplinarity of women's studies; further, it examines whether this is posed as a strength in terms of institutional openness of boundaries, or as a denial of academic legitimacy based on the perceived incoherence in the content of degree programmes.

Having been located as a student in the earliest degree programmes in Delhi within a university premised on interdisciplinarity and a pioneering women's studies research institution, these questions have much to do with the incessant concern that many of us, as students of women's studies, have with questions of disciplinary status and interdisciplinary training. The overwhelming concern of the field with these questions can be gauged by the range and depth of the reflections of students cited as evidence in this chapter. Thus, the reflections here do not seek to define or map out the contours of interdisciplinarity in women's studies but rather the meanings that the claim to interdisciplinarity holds for women's studies and how it structures various facets of degree programmes.

Not Just Interdisciplinary: Shifting Identifications of the Field

That women's studies is inexorably tied to the idea of interdisciplinarity is well accepted.[5] In the Indian context, archival material strongly indicates that in the founding phase, this was the primary and salient marker of women's studies as an academic field. In the conference and policy documents that record the incipient frameworks of setting up the field, it is argued that women's studies should be set up with reference to interdisciplinary fields like area studies, population studies, development studies and so on (Desai, Mazumdar and Bhansali 2003; SNDT Women's University 1981; University of Delhi

1985). The repeated reference to the ghettoisation of area studies in these documents, as an indication of the failure of the model of attaching interdisciplinary fields to existing disciplinary departments, is central to the idea of institutional autonomy for women's studies. This culminated in the UGC-driven model of Women's Studies Centres that has determined much of the institutional possibilities of women's studies in the Indian context. Thus, WSCs were set up with the idea that institutional autonomy would enable intellectual interdisciplinary interventions.

In contrast, in the American context (from where the term 'women's studies' was first borrowed),[6] women's studies was modelled on Black/Ethnic Studies, that is, fields of study based on identity (see, for instance, Showalter 1971).

It is significant then that in its early stages in India, women's studies—in response to the adverse impact of development policies on 'poor and rural' women—shifted the focus of research almost entirely to the working woman.[7] The stated aim of women's studies as an interdisciplinary field in higher education was to use the research produced to intervene in all disciplines as a critical perspective. However, in the first two decades, the intervention within disciplines could not but be limited by the fact that women's studies research was development-focused and largely conducted within economic frameworks.[8] Highlighting the fundamental contradiction in the founding mandate, Mary John argues that for women's studies,

> its mandate *not* to develop into a new field works *against* women's studies' inter- and trans-disciplinary mode of enquiry. It is not obvious how women's studies was meant to intervene within the existing structures of higher education, when, as everyone knows, the university system is not just organized around discrete disciplines, but is also deeply hierarchical across disciplines, with the sciences at the top of the hierarchy, economics further down, and the lower rungs of the ladder occupied by other social sciences and humanities. (John 2004: 26, emphasis in original)

This becomes evident when an overview of the courses offered across the 1980s indicates that curriculum development and teaching did in fact occur along disciplinary lines.[9]

While the 'autonomy–integration' debates in the American context (see Bowles and Duelli Klein 1983) emerged within a different history of institutionalisation, a similar trend about departmental status and possibilities of interdisciplinary teaching is noted by Judith Allen and Sally Kitch (1998). They argue that denial of departmental status to women's studies in order to effect integration within the disciplines and develop interdisciplinarity ironically resulted in the development of women's studies along disciplinary lines. The development of women's studies along integrationist principles is deemed a 'marginalised organisational strategy' by them (Allen and Kitch 1998: 290). Therefore, they argue for interdisciplinary PhD training in women's studies and corresponding departmental structures.

The push for women's studies as a teaching field in the Indian context did have much to do with its legitimisation as an academic field. At the turn of the twenty-first century, concerns about the reproduction of the field began to emerge (John 2002). Centres like the one at University A, after running for over a decade and offering short-term courses, strongly felt the need for students of their own (T1, interview, 16 January 2016). Although many in the field agreed that institutional reproduction is crucial to the survival of the field, there were differences over whether MA degrees in women's studies were feasible or only research degrees should be offered (T2, interview, 9 September 2017).

Moving away from the founding mandate, independent teaching courses and degrees began to spurt unevenly in the 1990s and degree programmes have emerged in a concerted manner in the past decade, since some scholars and WSCs felt the need to develop a dedicated body of students. In relation to the questions I shall discuss subsequently, what I find most interesting about this phase is the fact that as women's studies has developed as a degree-granting teaching field, its position as an academic field based on social identity has come to the foreground, as I argue elsewhere.[10]

Delving into the centrality of social identity as the organising principle of the field is crucial since it helps determine how important the question of interdisciplinarity is to those located within women's studies, and the ways in which they reflect upon it. For instance, almost all the interviews with students in the first round of my fieldwork, that is, 50 per cent of the total interviews conducted, are entirely focused on questions of social location and language (besides employability, which is a consistent concern across the data). In the remaining 50 per cent, interdisciplinarity and the disciplinary status of women's studies finds some focus to correct for the earlier gap; even so, questions of interdisciplinarity figure strongly only amongst students in Universities D and E, and to some extent in University C. As a professor of another interdisciplinary field remarked, interdisciplinarity is complicated by political questions in women's studies. While other interdisciplinary fields have also moved towards some kind of canonisation, this becomes much more complex for women's studies because it also has to answer to an existing movement (T3, interview, 26 September 2016).

Based on discussions in these five programmes, the battles in women's studies seem much more profound around the questions of identity and the subject of women's studies—methods and theories are debated but location and language become the routes to debate the adequacy or inadequacy of theory and methodology.

Meanings of Interdisciplinarity

As women's studies as a teaching field comes to be increasingly characterised by identity-based object(s) of enquiry, in what ways does interdisciplinarity hold meanings for the field? As it turns out, since many of the reflections around the field are centred on social location and identity and what it spells for feminist theory, interdisciplinarity acquires largely institutional meanings without much reflection as to what it would translate into in terms of the academic content of women's studies degrees. Most students claim that they find their curriculum interdisciplinary, though it remains unclear what 'interdisciplinary' means in this context beyond being accessible to students from varied disciplinary trainings. If seen as a mode of facilitating the institutional movement of students and faculty across disciplines, the question of interdisciplinarity also becomes one of the institutional autonomy of the field. On the one hand, if the interdisciplinarity of women's studies is assumed to mean 'anyone can do it', it can lead to the de-legitimisation of autonomous women's studies institutional spaces.[11] On the other hand, in institutions where women's studies continues to be considered non-academic, the very idea that interdisciplinarity means that 'anyone can do it' can become its source of legitimacy and the rationale for its continued existence. Interdisciplinarity can then become the route through which women's studies can claim autonomous institutional space by denying intellectual distinctiveness—the idea that 'anyone can do it' implies it requires no specialised academic training. Interdisciplinarity in this case means that it accommodates research of various disciplines, in contradiction to its critical function of questioning disciplinary frameworks.

The vast amount of theorisation on interdisciplinarity that has emerged globally attempts to engage with its various dimensions and meanings.[12] While the array of debates on how to build concepts and definitions of interdisciplinarity is too wide to enter here, for the questions I seek to raise the fundamental problem is whether interdisciplinarity is an amalgamation of disciplines, or if it seeks to dismantle the idea of disciplines by transcending disciplinary boundaries. As discussed earlier, the founding vision suggested that women's studies, through its interdisciplinary character, would break through the existing structures of disciplines. Contemporary students, however, largely understand its interdisciplinary character as a mix of disciplinary traditions—many of them use outsider/insider metaphors to argue that in relation to the curriculum, everyone is an outsider at some point (S1, interview, 30 May 2017). These questions remain unresolved, but it is evident that 'interdisciplinary' is defined by its distinction to a discipline. In my discussions with students and teachers, I found that the meanings of interdisciplinarity for women's studies—whether in terms of claims of achieving it or failing to do so—are in relation to perceptions of what constitutes a discipline.

Questions around disciplines and the history of disciplinarity have been central to debates on higher education, as James Chandler (2004) points out in a set of prominent debates in the American context. One aspect of these debates has been to understand disciplines in terms of the institutional structures that they inhabit. As various scholars have argued, the division into departments is a demand that arises with institutionalisation of knowledge in the university and is therefore closely linked to questions of academic identities and employability.[13] Following the arguments that disciplines are an answer to institutionalisation of knowledge, that is, the question of disciplines is actually one of departments, interdisciplinarity appears to be an answer to the problem of institutionalisation. Interdisciplinarity, then, has also to be read in terms of institutionalisation itself—as one teacher of women's studies remarked, within the history of women's studies, the urge to be interdisciplinary is at the core of resistance to institutionalise as a discipline. Thus in the 1990s, interdisciplinarity of women's studies was understood as seeking to question disciplines, not knowledge building as a discipline in its own right (T4, interview, 19 September 2016).

As mentioned earlier, the rationale behind having Women's Studies Centres, as opposed to being attached to departments, was to avoid the ghettoisation that interdisciplinary fields prior to women's studies had faced (University of Delhi 1985). It is the failure of institutional structures of the university to create space for new fields that the idea of 'interdisciplinarity' seeks to address. It seems that the intellectual meanings and practice of interdisciplinarity did not find much reflection, which is why the field seems to have a label which no one can define adequately (as is the case with interdisciplinarity in general). The move to confer degrees (and now to form departments in some instances) indicates demands for disciplinary status: not necessarily being a discipline but the institutional status that disciplines and departments carry.

The question of departmentalisation is one closely linked to employability, that is, disciplinary/departmental identities define possibilities of employment within higher education. It is for this reason that questions of interdisciplinarity become significant for students at the level of graduate research, and within the MA programme for students who seek to undertake research degrees.

The narratives emerging from the five programmes under study suggest that interdisciplinarity when accepted and celebrated becomes a question of 'lack of boundaries' institutionally; and when it is denigrated or rejected or when women's studies is found to not live up to it, the rejection centres on the 'lack of boundaries' intellectually. The following subsections will attempt to discuss these ideas in some detail through the voices of students and teachers.

Of Open Doors: Interdisciplinarity as Institutional Fluidity

The most obvious understanding of women's studies as an interdisciplinary academic field is centred on the institutional manifestations of its interdisciplinarity: the supposedly open boundaries that do not exercise rigidity in allowing entry, unlike disciplines.

For students seeking to enter women's studies at the research level (that is, those who do not hold a Master's degree in women's studies), interdisciplinarity offers an entry point and the lack of boundaries, along with what students term a more open space for exploring difficult, more political research questions that do not find space elsewhere. Here again, interdisciplinarity imbues women's studies degrees with the ability to transcend boundaries and structures of permissible modes of enquiry in academic institutions. For instance, two research students from University D describe their choice of a women's studies research degree as the answer to their search for an academic space where they could fit research that was not accepted by their departments, while holding on to their disciplinary training (interviews, S2, 7 October 2016; S3, 28 October 2016).

As a research degree, women's studies can simultaneously be a 'residual' space and an 'interdisciplinary' space that students seek in order to pursue particular research questions; in other words, interdisciplinarity is not necessarily methodological, merely *institutional*. When students see the strength of women's studies in this openness to different perspectives and frameworks, its lack of boundaries is central to their understanding of the field. However, they tend to define the field by what is it *not*: there is no agreement on what the field *is*.

Further, students seeking employment in higher education also frame the institutional meanings of interdisciplinarity in terms of questions of disciplinary/departmental identity and employability. In terms of employability, research students have a range of positions. For those seeking to break away from their parent disciplines, women's studies as a place of refuge for more feminist questions does not necessarily offer better employability. Their 'interdisciplinary' training in this instance becomes a disadvantage as it is interpreted to be a lack of expertise: they neither have advanced training in their parent disciplines, nor the 'basics' and 'foundations' of women's studies that they argue are required to teach in the field. A PhD student in such a situation shared that she did not feel she was 'trained' in women's studies, and that it would be difficult to find employment because the Indian higher education system is still structured along disciplines (S4, interview, 19 September 2016). However, students who are rooted in their parent disciplines and would prefer to be employed in the respective departments find that having a mainstream Master's degree is an advantage as it promises better employment possibilities. In relation to this dilemma, a teacher advises students to acquire their Master's in a mainstream discipline and their research degrees in women's studies to improve prospects of employability in both kinds of departments (T5, interview, 5 August 2016).

For MA students seeking non-academic employment avenues, the appeal of interdisciplinarity is that it offers flexibility. Thus the laments of incoherence of academic content and grounding, which the next sub-section will highlight, are not significant for this set of students. Celebrating interdisciplinarity as a glorious transcendence of mainstream structures of knowledge, a student underlines that her appreciation of women's studies' tendency to break epistemic boundaries is tied to the fact that she is not seeking an academic career. At the same time, she feels that those seeking boundaries cannot survive women's studies as she understands it (S5, interview, 28 April 2016).

The question of employment and the centrality of interdisciplinarity for employment questions in women's studies also necessitate thinking about the academic backgrounds of women's studies teachers in these institutions. As most of the currently existing faculty of women's studies do not hold women's studies degrees, their institutional location is determined by the interdisciplinary nature of the field. Often, teachers then stake their claim to women's studies departments by framing women's studies as having 'no core' and hence requiring other disciplines to exist.

Therefore, this institutional fluidity attributed to women's studies as an interdisciplinary field is premised on the idea that there is no core training that is required to undertake research or teaching in women's studies on account of its interdisciplinarity. It is this idea of the absence of a core and boundaries of academic content, which disciplines supposedly have, that works against the field.

Of Seeking Ground: Interdisciplinarity as Intellectual 'Incoherence'

While the emphasis on women's studies as being interdisciplinary has much to do with institutional questions of field formation, amongst these five programmes, in general, the failure of women's studies to be interdisciplinary—or even the rejection of interdisciplinarity as a useful framework for women's studies—usually has to do with its academic content as a teaching field. As the following discussion will illustrate, students usually find a sense of coherence or grounding lacking within coursework, while teachers locate this lack in the frameworks of research that students deploy.

Women's studies degrees exist within mainstream university structures and hence despite pedagogical innovations, are bound by existing academic requirements. Sharmila Rege argues in the context of the WSC at Savitribai Phule Pune University (SPPU),

> As the Centre was made autonomous in 1998, the experiences of sudden dislocation from a disciplinary dwelling confirmed that there are indeed few real institutional frameworks and procedures to make interdisciplinarity work within university structures. Autonomy or integration within disciplines is at best an academic debate. In practice, most WSCs are required to make the 'choice' of either 'dissolving' within disciplinary regimes of the university

> system or 'stand alone' without any possibilities of collaboration with teaching/research programmes in the disciplines. (Rege 2011: 61)

Coursework

Thus, the women's studies degree attempts to offer interdisciplinary training in feminist thought and methods within the structural bounds of a conventional curriculum. While standardisation and canonisation have often been considered undesirable in women's studies, it has also meant that syllabi and pedagogy are often more dependent on the individual or group of scholars designing and teaching courses than would be the case in other disciplines. This also has to do with the fact that thus far those teaching women's studies by and large do not hold degrees in women's studies, so disciplinary backgrounds of faculty members become significant. While interdisciplinarity has become a catchword, a teacher in University D finds that in practice most people work on gender using their disciplinary training, rather than picking up the methodologies of other disciplines. Thus the women's studies department often becomes limited by the disciplinary training of its corresponding faculty members (T6, interview, 7 October 2016).

As many students discuss, the disciplinary background of the teacher significantly alters how any course may be taught. The course on 'Feminist Theory', which is a standard component of every MA and MPhil. course, varies greatly in content and pedagogy—there is no standard set of thinkers/ideas taught in the different versions of the course across institutions. Further, students who have been taught the same course by, say, a historian and a literature scholar have completely different understandings of what they term 'the basics' of the course. This effectively means that the very framework of the course can change significantly from year to year. In other words, the practice of interdisciplinarity in any curriculum is determined by the composition of the faculty and their disciplinary training and research interests (T7, interview, 18 February 2016). Interdisciplinarity usually amounts to a mix of readings, but pedagogically teachers are limited to their disciplinary trainings, as one research student argues. The disciplinary background of the teacher becomes dominant in their teaching (S6, interview, 27 June 2017). It is thus also a lament of literature students that the interdisciplinarity of women's studies is largely social science based and excludes humanities almost entirely (S7, interview, 5 May 2016).

Since the disciplinary backgrounds of faculty have much to do with the content and structure of a curriculum, it can appear to students that women's studies as a field is fragmented. In certain instances, students argue that individual courses have much to offer in content and depth but the overall coursework for their degree is not 'coherent' and leaves them 'ungrounded': students frequently use the terms 'lack of grounding', 'incoherent', 'fragmented', and 'patchwork'. Across programmes, some students find feminist theory courses too scattered in terms of themes, where they do not gain depth in any theme or a sense of coherence (interviews, S8, 1 August 2017; S9, 9 June 2017).[14]

Therefore, the data appears to suggest that the teaching of feminist theory courses is not interdisciplinary but rather more multidisciplinary and theme-based, where disciplinary perspectives do not speak to each other (interviews, S6, 27 June 2017; S10, 11 August 2017; S11, 25 November 2017). Further, the attempt to teach the idea of multiple feminisms can be internalised by students as implying that feminism and feminist theory have no foundational grounding. Thus the political and theoretical failures of feminism are located in this perceived lack of boundaries and/or fixed foundations. The combination of multidisciplinary tendencies, varying disciplinary training of the faculty, and the disciplinary entrenchment of students whereby they seek 'foundations', results in a situation where it can appear to students that women's studies as a field is fragmented. The courses were simultaneously found to be overloaded and incoherent, and essentially feminist theory courses face the 'problem of doing too much' (interviews, S9, 9 June 2017; S6, 27 June 2017; S11, 25 November 2017; S12, 24 November 2017; S13, 24 August 2017).

Thus, one challenge with feminist theory is multidisciplinary overload and the weight of rigour that it carries. Linked to this is the other dilemma that theory brings in—how to engage with critique without being reduced to a derivative status. Teachers reported having to constantly re-work courses in terms of how best to engage with teaching 'originals' and the 'feminist critique' work/texts—this adds to all the pressures of overload.

The sense of incoherence also comes from a certain disciplinary entrenchment of the students wherein I find students looking for genealogical trajectories of thought (yet again more a feature of research degrees than Master's degrees, where students are more concerned with practice or applicability). Many argue that they need to read the original texts and traditions of thought, thereby treating feminist thought as derivative. For instance, as part of the MPhil. coursework at University E, some batches of students read *The Sexual Contract* (1988) by Carole Pateman, and thus they constantly refer to political science as a desirable academic background, or the need to read Rousseau. Further, some teachers (usually those with some training in women's studies) argue that women's studies must constantly operate in a mode of internal critique (interviews, T8, 27 April 2016; T9, 8 September 2016). Students, however, are sometimes left feeling that women's studies is 'only critique' and does not offer them theoretical grounding, leaving them uncertain about their academic training (S6, interview, 27 June 2017).

In response to these problems, some teachers have altered their courses, particularly introductory courses, to discuss the basics of feminism and gender first as opposed to deconstructing them (T9, interview, 21 August 2017). On the other hand, some teachers insisted on teaching critical analysis and the politics of knowledge production instead of transacting information. They framed their courses as attempting to teach how knowledge about dominant paradigms is produced rather than the paradigms themselves (interviews, T7, 13 February 2016; T8, 27 April 2016). As a Master's student put it, in women's studies courses, students were made to question the assumptions behind ideas/concepts, and not accept anything as canonical (S13, interview, 24 August 2017).

Thus the frame of reference for such critiques is disciplinary training, which is believed to provide some expertise. A research student ascribed her uncertainty to her experience that interdisciplinary academic training is not 'rigorous' in ways that normative disciplines are because they have fixed frameworks and methods (S14, interview, 26 May 2017).

In this regard, some MA students in Universities B and E argue that they would choose to go for a second Master's degree in a 'core discipline' (interviews, S15, 16 August 2017; S16, 29 November 2017); from MPhil. students' perspective, they report having acquired some specialised training, but for their PhD degrees, they would rather return to their parent disciplines, as discussed in the previous section.

Perceptions of lack of grounding have much to do with the question of feminist methodology and its significance in a women's studies degree—in some locations, the adequacy of feminist methodology stands questioned, even extending to debates on whether the degree should have an entire course on feminist methodology or not. Often, feminist methodology courses are rendered difficult or impossible because the field is interdisciplinary (since it is not a discipline with a distinctive methodology of 'its own'). There was considerable ambiguity amongst women's studies teachers about feminist methodology. Some teachers argued that feminist scholars have not worked towards building their own methodological traditions; rather, feminist research has relied on methods borrowed from mainstream disciplines (interviews, T2, 9 September 2017; T9, 21 August 2017; T10, 26 October 2017; T11, 3 January 2018). On the other hand some programmes, such as the one at University B, emphasise that the feminist method is central to the women's studies research degree and the potential for interdisciplinarity in women's studies degrees is located in methodological questions. The idea is that it is through a shift in methodologies and by engaging with other disciplinary traditions in ways that make them more reflexive that interdisciplinary work can be attempted (T4, interview, 19 September 2016).

A significant proportion of students of women's studies were often not convinced about feminist methodology. Master's students were not focused on the methodological and epistemological challenges of feminism as their focus was on feminist 'questions'. Often when students rejected feminist methodology, it was because they did not engage with underlying feminist philosophical traditions and reduced the debate to bare methods and techniques. Thus, they claimed that feminist methodology only goes a bit further in bringing in 'lived experience', 'ethics and sensitivity' and so on (interviews, S14, 26 May 2017; S17, 6 September 2017; S18, 6 September 2017; S19, 29 June 2017). Students who had entered at the PhD level with the understanding of women's studies as 'open' and welcoming all kinds of research were the least convinced about feminist methodology. In their view, the interdisciplinarity of women's studies should include methods from various disciplinary traditions. So while they were clear that their research could not be conducted within any mainstream discipline and needed feminist research expertise, at the same time they did not agree that there is a distinct feminist methodology, and believed that other disciplines have the same methods (interviews, S2, 7 October 2016; S3, 28 October 2016; S20, 8 June 2017; S21, 20 July 2017; S22, 8 September 2017).

Another set of students, however, insisted that feminist methodological training is needed to undertake research in women's studies, since it seeks to question how knowledge is mediated by location, including disciplinary location (interviews, S12, 24 November 2017; S13, 24 August 2017; S23, 21 November 2017; S24, 6 June 2017; S25, 7 September 2017; S26, 11 September 2017; S27, 11 September 2017; S28, 27 November 2017; S29, 29 November 2017; S30, 13 February 2016).

In this regard, I think it is useful to reflect on responses to the Feminist Research Methods/Methodology (FRM) course, a much-debated component for all MA and MPhil. courses under study. As setting up teaching programmes reflects the effort to establish the academic bent of women's studies (distinct from outreach), all five programmes strongly emphasise academic rigour in general and a research-oriented bent to the MA degrees. Students of women's studies at the MA level are usually a mix of those seeking to undertake research degrees and those seeking employment in the development sector, media, and other domains (the latter are found to form a higher proportion: 60 to 80 per cent depending on the size of the classroom). The FRM courses in the MA degree, then, are often rendered superfluous by students, who sometimes argue that they should be oriented towards teaching methods that can be useful in the field (S31, interview, 7 June 2017). Given this varying orientation of students and consequently, the ambiguous position that an FRM course holds in the MA curriculum, the course essentially becomes about balancing the teaching of feminist methodological debates while getting across the basics of what would constitute methods of social research. In some programmes, the women's studies faculty have often had to reformulate the course in accordance with the requirements of students across different batches. In some instances, teaching research methods is favoured because, as one teacher put it, epistemological questions were often lost on Master's students (T9, interview, 21 August 2017). At times, the strategy was to teach separate courses on research methods and feminist methodology (interviews, T12, 25 October 2017; S25, 7 September 2017; S32, 22 November 2017).

The Methods course at the MPhil. level, and indeed the MPhil. women's studies degree as a whole, throws up even more interesting questions. Since the MPhil. degree has been phased out under the National Education Policy 2020, these contentions about disciplinary training and interdisciplinarity in women's studies MPhil. courses bring out all the more strongly the possibilities of MPhil. degrees acting as bridges to enable interdisciplinary graduate research. The FRM courses at the level of graduate research in these programmes highlight the plethora of dilemmas and debates within and among their ideas of what a feminist methodological training should constitute. The MPhil. coursework at University B, for instance, has courses that trace genealogies of dominant schools of thought and then engage with their feminist critiques, and it is this aspect that students highlight the most; the coursework at University E is more thematic, not discipline-based, which one of the teachers in the programme argues is an indication that the course attempts to build women's studies as a discipline as opposed to critique (T9, interview, 21 August 2017).

The second question structuring research degree curriculum is whether the MPhil. coursework is based on the assumption of an MA (or any prior) training in women's studies. For instance at Universities A and B, students argue that the MPhil. coursework presumes prior training in women's studies and thus is focused on methodology. In the research programme at University E, students have found that the MPhil. coursework attempts to 'bridge' the 'gaps' created by or resulting from the claim to interdisciplinarity, by training students in the basics of women's studies as well as methodology simultaneously. The significance of this question lies in the debate about the disciplinary grounding of the women's studies research student.

Graduate research

Along with coursework being perceived as incoherent and inadequately grounded and structured, the idea of graduate research being fragmented is the other significant point of contention where the interdisciplinary potential of women's studies stands questioned. While students find their research to be entirely disconnected from each other's work at times, the idea that the lack of grounding and coherence is rooted in interdisciplinarity itself also emerged in discussions with teachers of women's studies, with reference to the disciplinary/interdisciplinary backgrounds of graduate students and the nature of research produced in their respective programmes.

As MA degrees in women's studies continue to proliferate, amongst the programmes under study where such degrees have been in place for almost a decade, there is ambiguity about the MA interdisciplinary training—yet again based on the idea of the lack of 'disciplinary grounding'. One set of teachers argues that students with MA degrees in women's studies are better oriented to the corresponding research degrees (T5, interview, 5 August 2016), whereas others find that the MA equips students with conceptual vocabulary but they still require methodological training (interviews, T8, 27 April 2016; T12, 25 October 2017). However, the requirement of methodological training is true of students entering any research degree in general. Yet, some teachers argue that the interdisciplinary training of the women's studies Master's degree places students at a disadvantage at the research level. With reference to the MPhil. degree, one teacher argues that students with their Master's in women's studies struggle the most in developing a research methodology because the course is very 'loose' structurally. In her view, disciplines give students a definite framework to approach an issue and thus women's studies does not train students for advanced research (T13, interview, 6 October 2017). However, a research student with an MA in women's studies argues that it is a question of whether the Master's training of a student has been in interdisciplinary or disciplinary traditions, not whether it is in women's studies or not (S8, interview, 1 August 2017).

In general, given that interdisciplinary methods are not well-defined, research degrees in women's studies continue to face the danger of becoming residual, catch-all spaces. Often, the larger problem that teachers face is of students treating interdisciplinary feminist methodology as the absence of a rigorous framework. The danger then, according to a teacher, is much more of scholars not having *any* framework at all and eclectically drawing on various frameworks without grounding themselves in the methodology of women's studies (T1, interview, 16 January 2016).

To deal with these methodological dilemmas, the MPhil.–PhD coursework also focuses on consistently making students think about why their question is feminist or relevant to 'women's studies', and to try and understand how they can use their disciplinary training in meaningful critical ways instead of discarding it. The question of whether and how research is feminist is also felt as a pressure by students in women's studies research programmes at Universities D and E, where they find that interdisciplinarity holds at the level of entry, but within the research degree, certain unspoken boundaries exist. So, as a research student points out, the graduate research produced usually qualifies as multidisciplinary at best, yet students do feel that there is a pressure for research to be feminist, and a discomfort with research that is entrenched in disciplinary methods (S9, interview, 9 June 2017). Teachers did not consider graduate research to fit the requirements of training in women's studies when students presented research that focused on gender questions but within the theoretical and methodological frameworks of their parent disciplines. Further, most students in this research programme argue that their research is disconnected from each other and the claim to interdisciplinarity does not translate to students from different disciplinary backgrounds being able to access each other's work, as there is 'no common ground' to research produced by graduate students even within the same batch.

Conclusion

Read together, the narratives of students suggest a paradoxical situation where women's studies is too theoretical but has no theory of its own, too rigorous yet not grounded like disciplines. Thus the arguments about lack of boundaries, which seek to validate or reject interdisciplinarity as a defining characteristic of women's studies as an academic field, emerge from the perceived contrast with disciplines. That interdisciplinarity lacks clear definitions in general and is largely a response to the problem of departmentalisation is fairly evident; for women's studies, the meanings are yet more complex when interdisciplinarity is interpreted as the absence of rigid boundaries of the object of enquiry and is extended to mean an openness to more 'political' questions. In seeking theoretical training to answer political questions, the methodological premises of women's studies in taught programmes and graduate research tend to become insignificant at times or lose relevance. In a policy environment where interdisciplinarity is increasingly gaining favour as being the route to more flexible knowledge models and internationalised higher education systems, some sections of women's studies are beginning to question whether it has much academic meaning.

Of course these manifestations of the inadequacies of women's studies in its interdisciplinarity have much to do with those designing curricula and teaching courses, since many of the teachers of women's studies are trained within mainstream disciplinary traditions. Students of women's studies are increasingly beginning to argue that the critical training offered by women's studies is necessary in order to teach women's studies, and further argue for the closing of disciplinary boundaries. The question of the interdisciplinarity of women's studies will become yet more complex as a generation of scholars exclusively trained in women's studies begins to emerge in significant numbers.

Notes

1. See the Report of the 'Committee to Advise on Renovation and Rejuvenation of Higher Education' (2010), brought out by the Yash Pal Committee, which was set up by the Ministry of Human Resource Development (MHRD) under the UPA government; the Report of the 'Committee for Evolution of the New Education Policy' (2016a and b) brought out by the T. S. R. Subramanian Committee set up by the MHRD; and the report titled 'Some Inputs for Draft National Education Policy 2016' brought out by the MHRD under the present government. These reports equate excellence with internationalisation and new models of knowledge that will move beyond disciplines. For instance, the Yash Pal Committee Report in its recommendations for 'World Class Universities' repeatedly argues against disciplinary divisions and promotes interdisciplinarity, stating that 'new knowledge and new insights have often originated at the boundaries of disciplines' (MHRD 2010: 2).

2. This chapter has been drawn from my ongoing doctoral research.

3. The nomenclature of the degrees at these institutions varies between women's studies, gender studies, and combinations of the two. At University A, the MA is offered in Gender, Culture and Development Studies, the MPhil. degree is titled Women's/Gender Studies and the PhD is in Women's Studies, while the Centre is still a Women's Studies Centre and most students identify as 'students of women's studies'; at University E, the MA degree is in Gender Studies while the MPhil. and PhD degrees are Women's and Gender Studies. At the remaining three institutions, the respective degrees offered are titled Women's Studies. However, for the purposes of this chapter I shall use 'women's studies' to evoke the name of the field as it was first used in the Indian context. The women's studies/gender studies debate is extremely significant in the present moment but remains beyond the scope of this chapter.

4. As ethical concerns of maintaining anonymity are critical, the names of the institutions have been anonymised as Universities A, B, C, D, and E. Individuals have also been anonymised: instead of providing pseudonyms, 'T1, T2…' have been used for teachers, and 'S1, S2…' for students.

5. According to pioneering figure Vina Mazumdar, '[b]y its very nature, women's studies could not be imprisoned within the formal boundaries of the established disciplines' (1994: 44). Some teachers at University E discuss how, despite being one amongst a number of other interdisciplinary fields, the burden to 'prove' interdisciplinarity is experienced disproportionately by the Gender Studies programme. Similar arguments are raised by women's studies students in University B, another institution where largely interdisciplinary degrees are offered.

6. The histories of the first university-based women's studies research centre at SNDT Women's University, Mumbai, acknowledge that 'women's studies' originated in the US and indeed the Centre was engaged in significant intellectual exchange with American women's studies in the late 1970s to develop curricula and teaching models (see Kosambi 1998; Krishnaraj 1999; RCWS 1989).

7. Mazumdar and Sharma (1979), in a review of women's studies in the 1970s, reflect on how the ICSSR mandate directed research in women's studies to focus on women and development as it was felt that knowledge about poor women who had thus far been 'invisible' was urgently required. Desai and Patel (1989) find that the focus on development-related concerns was almost to the exclusion of other concerns, including violence, which became a significant concern for the contemporary women's movement.

8. Kumud Sharma (1994) argues that the research on women, work, and development in the founding period was largely conducted from economic perspectives. Desai and Patel (1989) also comment in their review of research in women's studies over the 1970s and 1980s that the concern with rural and poor women and the question of work, usually in an economic and statistical sense, was dominant in these studies.

9. Some collections of the outlines of women's studies courses in the 1980s illustrate that the space women's studies could find was usually an elective or sub-topics within courses and the frameworks of these courses were entrenched in the respective disciplines (see Patwa 1985; Sanjanwala 1988).

10. In my doctoral thesis, I discuss the evolution of women's studies in India, with the establishment of degree programmes, as an identity knowledge field.

11. One recent instance that comes to mind is that of JNU, where the women's studies refresher course was assigned to another centre in the name of interdisciplinarity. See Arunima (2017).

12. Interdisciplinary Studies, in the North American context, is an institutionalised field with departments and degrees. Its trajectory of institutionalisation has changed over time, with shifts in the legitimacy of disciplines and interdisciplinarity as organising principles of knowledge. Julie Thompson Klein is a pioneering scholar located in one such department (see Klein 1990; 1996). Peter Weingart, another pioneer in this field, is a German sociologist of science (see Weingart and Stehr 2000).

13. Chandler (2009), however, cautions that disciplines cannot be reduced to institutional structures alone as that would mean 'to deny the possibility that a disciplinary system can evolve beyond the structure—that of the academic departments, for example—that is meant to administer it' (2009:

734). In an important cross-context volume on interdisciplinarity, Stephen Turner (2000) also defines disciplines in terms of departments, focusing on their degree-granting power and questions of employability. Chandler (2009) also points out that the question of disciplinarity has much to do with academic identities.

14. This perspective has either to do with the spread of themes across traditions of thought and method, which are not accessible to them, or the scale of readings which, being from different disciplinary traditions, are not within grasp of all students. Sometimes it also has to do with the fact that different instructors have different approaches where shared courses leave students with a sense of fragmentation.

References

Allen, Judith A., and Sally L. Kitch. 1998. 'Disciplined by Disciplines? The Need for an Interdisciplinary Research Mission in Women's Studies'. *Feminist Studies* 24 (2): 275–299.

Arunima, G. 2017. 'JNU's Women's Studies Course Moved from Centre for Women's Studies'. *The Wire*, 8 October. Available at https://thewire.in/education/jnus-womens-studies-course-moved-from-centre-for-womens-studies (accessed November 2023).

Bowles, Gloria, and Renate Duelli Klein (eds). 1983. *Theories of Women's Studies*. Boston: Routledge and Kegan Paul.

Brown, Wendy. 2008. 'The Impossibility of Women's Studies'. In *Women's Studies on the Edge*, Joan Wallach Scott (ed.): 17–38. Durham: Duke University Press.

Chandler, James. 2004. 'Critical Disciplinarity'. *Critical Inquiry* 30 (2): 355–360.

______. 2009. 'Introduction: Doctrines, Disciplines, Discourses, Departments'. *Critical Inquiry* 35 (4): 729–746.

Desai, Neera, and Vibhuti Patel. 1989. *Critical Review of Researches in Women's Studies, 1975–88*. Mumbai: SNDT Women's University.

Desai, Neera, Vina Mazumdar, and Kamalini Bhansali. 2003. 'From Women's Education to Women's Studies: A Long Drawn Struggle for Legitimacy and Influence'. In *Narratives from the Women's Studies Family*, Devaki Jain and Pam Rajput (eds): 44–77. New Delhi: Sage.

Friedman, Susan Stanford. 1998. '(Inter)Disciplinarity and the Question of the Women's Studies Ph.D'. *Feminist Studies* 24 (2): 301–325.

John, Mary E. 2002. 'Introduction to a Round-table Discussion'. *Indian Journal of Gender Studies* 9 (2): 203–207.

______. 2004. 'Country Paper—India'. In *Women's/Gender Studies in Asia-Pacific*, Philip Bergstrom (ed.): 17–48. Bangkok: UNESCO Asia and Pacific Regional Bureau for Education.

______. 2011. 'The Problem'. *Seminar* 624. Available at https://web.archive.org/web/20200719073216/http://www.india-seminar.com/2011/624/624_the_problem.htm (accessed November 2023).

Klein, Julie Thompson. 1990. *Interdisciplinarity: History, Theory, and Practice*. Detroit: Wayne State University Press.

______. 1996. *Crossing Boundaries: Knowledge, Disciplinarities and Interdisciplinarities*. London: University Press of Virginia.

Kosambi, Meera. 1998. 'Country Paper on India'. In Proceedings of 'Building Women's Studies Curriculum in Asia', 26–28 March: 119–136. Seoul: EWHA Women's University.

Krishnaraj, Maithreyi. 1999. 'Women's Studies Centre at SNDT Women's University, Mumbai 1974–1999'. In Papers presented at UGC Workshop on Publication of Volume on Women's Studies, Chandigarh, April 15–17, 1999. Chandigarh.

Mazumdar, Vina. 1994. 'Women's Studies and the Women's Movement in India: An Overview'. *Women's Studies Quarterly* 22 (3/4): 42–54.

Mazumdar, Vina, and Kumud Sharma. 1979. 'Women's Studies: New Perceptions and the Challenges'. *Economic and Political Weekly* 14 (3): 113–120.

Ministry of Human Resource Development. 2010. *Report of the 'Committee to Advise on Renovation and Rejuvenation of Higher Education' (Yash Pal Committee Report)*. New Delhi: Government of India.

______. 2016a. *Report of the 'Committee for Evolution of the New Education Policy' (T.S.R. Subramanian Committee Report)*. New Delhi: Government of India.

______. 2016b. *Some Inputs for Draft National Education Policy 2016*. New Delhi: Government of India.

Patwa, Subhadra. 1985. *Women's Studies Centres in India*. Bombay: Research Centre for Women's Studies.

Rege, Sharmila. 2003. 'Introduction'. In *Sociology of Gender: The Challenge of Feminist Sociological Knowledge*: 1–49. New Delhi: Sage.

______. 2011. 'Women's Studies Since the 1990s: Mapping New Conjectures, Challenges and Strategies'. In *Insights and Interventions: Essays in Honour of Uma Chakravarti*, Kumkum Roy (ed.): 39–74. Delhi: Primus Books.

Research Centre for Women's Studies (RCWS). 1989. *Planning Women's Studies in Indian Universities: Proceedings of the National Level Workshop of UGC Supported Women's Studies Centres and Cells*. 23–24 October, organised by RCWS. Mumbai: RCWS.

Sanjanwala, Jyotsna. 1988. *Building a Curriculum*. Contribution to Women's Studies Series. Bombay: RCWS.

Sharma, Kumud. 1994. 'Women's Studies in India: Academia and Action'. In *The India-Canada Relationship: Exploring the Political, Economic and Cultural Dimensions*, J. S. Grewal and Hugh Johnston (eds): 331–343. New Delhi: Sage.

Showalter, Elaine. 1971. 'Introduction: Teaching about Women, 1971'. In *Female Studies IV: Teaching about Women*, Elaine Showalter and Carol Ohmann (eds): i–xii. Pittsburg, Pennsylvania: Know Inc.

SNDT Women's University. 1981. *Report of the First National Conference on Women's Studies, 20–24 April*. Bombay: SNDT Women's University.

Sreenivas, Deepa. 2015. 'Between Politics and Discipline: Gender Studies in an Institutional Setting'. *Indian Journal of Gender Studies* 22 (2): 265–281.

Sreerekha, M. S. 2016. 'Whatever Happened to Women's Studies'. *Economic and Political Weekly* 51 (15): 64–68.

Tharu, Susie, and Tejaswini Niranjana. 1999. 'Problems for a Contemporary Theory of Gender'. In *Gender and Politics in India*, Nivedita Menon (ed.): 472–525. Delhi: Oxford University Press.

Turner, Stephen. 2000. 'What are Disciplines? And How is Interdisciplinarity Different?'. In *Practising Interdisciplinarity*, Peter Weingart and Nico Stehr (eds): 46–65. Toronto: University of Toronto Press.

University Grants Commission (UGC). 1986. *Guidelines for the Development of Women's Studies in Indian Universities and Colleges*. New Delhi: UGC.

______. 2012. *Twelfth Plan Guidelines: Development of Women's Studies in Indian Universities and Colleges & Capacity Building of Women Managers in Higher Education*. New Delhi: UGC.

University of Delhi. 1985. *Report of the Seminar on Perspectives and Organisation of Women's Studies Units in Indian Universities, April 21–23, 1985. Research Group on Women's Studies, Department of Political Science, University of Delhi*. New Delhi: University of Delhi.

Weingart, Peter. 2000. 'Interdisciplinarity: The Paradoxical Discourse'. In *Practising Interdisciplinarity*, Peter Weingart and Nico Stehr (eds): 25–41. Toronto: University of Toronto Press.

Weingart, Peter, and Nico Stehr (eds). 2000. *Practising Interdisciplinarity*. Toronto: University of Toronto Press.

Wiegman, Robyn. 2012. *Object Lessons*. Durham: Duke University Press.

5

In Defence of Indiscipline

Disciplining and Decentring Women's Studies in Non-metropolitan Tamil Nadu

Nithila Kanagasabai[1]

In February 2014, over twenty students and scholars from Bharathidasan University (BDU) in Tiruchirappalli, Tamil Nadu, participated and presented papers at the Fourteenth National Conference of the Indian Association for Women's Studies (IAWS) held at Guwahati, Assam. Most of them were in their mid-to-late twenties, hailed from villages near the main city of Tiruchirappalli, and were first-generation graduates. Many of them had chanced upon the discipline of women's studies a few years earlier through the recommendations of their mentors, or even because their families thought of it as a *safe* course[2] because it was mostly women who pursued the discipline. The Master's students were at the conference because they were planning to enrol in research degrees and were curious about a life in academia. The research scholars, already enrolled in MPhil. or PhD degrees, were there to present their research and also to acquaint themselves with the work of their peers and senior academics.

Academic narratives about women's studies in non-metropolitan centres frequently evince a deep-rooted anxiety about the disciplinary practices in such locations, since they are thought to focus more on extension activities that the State encourages, rather than prioritising the subversive potential of feminist epistemological endeavours (Anandhi and Swaminathan 2006). Writing in an IAWS newsletter a decade later, S. Anandhi (2017) places the growth of women's studies within the larger framework of higher education in Tamil Nadu. She points out that even as the field was gaining ground in the state, there was an increased focus on the vocationalisation of higher education and large-scale privatisation.[3] The former, she goes on to argue, resulted in the restructuring of courses—including women's studies—that the State deemed to be '...non-utility (non-merit) subjects':

> With these changes Women's Studies was no longer an intellectual project, but a marketable product that could fetch future possibilities of integrating women into the market economy. The assimilation of market ideas and co-option of women's studies by the state to realize its own objectives of women's empowerment brought in a unique trend in the institutionalization of Women's Studies in Tamil Nadu. (Anandhi 2017: 62)

In a bid to gain 'visibility and recognition', she writes, women's studies too has been vocationalised.

Mary E. John, writing in the same issue of the IAWS newsletter as S. Anandhi, notes that we are currently in an 'extraordinary' situation, wherein 'there has been massive privatisation in education in recent years.... [And]—side by side—a process of growing democratisation in the composition of student population' (2017: 67). She refers to the increased entry of women in institutions of higher education, but also to the implementation of reservations, resulting in the entry of more students belonging to marginalised caste and religious locations. Simultaneously, she clarifies the fact that *access to* higher education and *life experiences in* higher education are discrete, and though the former may be guaranteed by the state, the quality of the latter is dependent on sociocultural factors. It is in this context[4] of higher education, marked by discrepant developments—of vocationalisation, privatisation, and democratisation—both within the state of Tamil Nadu, and the country at large, that this chapter proposes an engagement with micro-negotiations along with attention to structural inequities.

S. Roy (2009: 341) argues that the present trend of anxiety about the depoliticisation of the women's movement or women's studies can be a read as a 'melancholic loss—a fetishized attachment to the past, and to past modes of knowledge, action and consciousness in ways that demand the generational reproduction of feminism rather than its renewal in times of perceived crisis'. She pays particular importance to women's studies as a discipline, arguing that it was always-already conceptualised as the intellectual arm of the Women's Movement, where research would be oriented towards action, a transformation at the ground level. The weakening of this 'originary' link has led to questioning of the politics of the discipline itself and its methods of knowledge production.

Feminist scholarship suggests that women's studies has alternatively been critiqued for being too theoretical (and so losing touch with ground realities), and too focused on field action (and consequently not producing knowledge that is subversive). Roy (2009) goes on to argue that this easy binary prevents internal or meta-critique central to the exercise of feminist theorising. Emphasising the need to go beyond the divisions of academia and activism, she posits the need to rethink the ways in which new relationships are produced, and how these in turn reconfigure preexisting relationships. This chapter is an attempt to reconsider the formations of women's studies within the country, focusing on the twin impulses of disciplining and decentring that animate discussions around women's studies pedagogy, while being sensitive to the ruptures and discontinuities within the disciplinary discourse in India.

Due to the growing number of Women's Studies Centres (WSCs) between 2007 and 2017,[5] there has been a shift in the composition of those accessing institutionalised women's studies in India, with increasing numbers of people from traditionally disadvantaged locations (with respect to class, caste, region, religion, and sexuality) entering the field. This needs to be examined as not simply a change in demography, but a radical change in the very texture of women's studies as an institutionalised discipline in Indian higher education. Thus, even as there is increased privatisation, there are also strong assertions of identity by students from marginalised social locations and a consequent attempt by both students and teachers of the discipline to evolve a political language of a highly self-reflexive women's studies paradigm, articulated both within the classroom and outside of it. This chapter argues that in this state of flux, an engagement with the experiences and situated knowledge of those involved in women's studies in non-metropolitan locations enables a critical reflection on not just the functioning of women's studies as both politics and discipline within this particular context, but also stands to offer a lens for a critical appraisal of the institutionalised discipline at large.

A Note on Methods Employed

This research employs narrative methods and focuses on WSCs in two universities in Tamil Nadu—Bharathidasan University (BDU) in Tiruchirappalli and Bharathiar University (BU) in Coimbatore. I first met a few students and scholars from BDU at the 2014 IAWS National Conference. Largely due to linguistic commonalities and the fact that we shared a hostel during the week-long conference, I happened to interact with them. At that point I was still an outsider to women's studies as my disciplinary training was in media and cultural studies. Although I was engaged in feminist scholarship, it was only a few months after the conference that I decided to apply and enrol in an MPhil. programme in women's studies. In a sense, it is with these peers that my journey to the discipline began. Over the course of 2015, I spoke with six Master's (MA) students, four research scholars, and one faculty member at Bharathidasan University. At Bharathiar University, I spoke with six MA students, four research scholars, and four faculty members. I also engaged in a focus group discussion with first-year MA students at both universities. The recorded conversations were translated and transcribed, and the first draft of this chapter was presented at the Fifteenth National Conference of IAWS in Chennai in 2017. Thus it would not be wrong to say that scholars from non-metropolitan locations and the IAWS have had a formative impact on my journey to and within the discipline.

In writing this chapter, I wanted to retain the names of the research participants for multiple reasons. Names are critical, for they are not just used in identifying the self, but because they speak of aspiration and cultural location. Scholars from these locations have been involved in research within the discipline of women's studies for more than a decade,[6] and yet their names are largely absent from the dominant discourse of women's studies, pointing to the hierarchies within the discipline. Research participants were well aware of this absence and in fact, pointed out the non-engagement of metropolitan women's studies with their scholarship. Sara Ahmed (2013) defines practices of citation as 'a rather successful reproductive technology, a way of reproducing the world around certain bodies'. Pointing to the foundational role that citational practices play in not just structuring, but also forming disciplines, and linking this to an embodied performance, she writes,

> When we think this question 'who appears?' we are asked a question about how spaces are occupied by certain bodies who get so used to their occupation that they don't even notice it. They are comfortable, like a body that sinks into a chair that has received its shape over time. To question who appears is to become the cause of discomfort. It is almost as if we have a duty not to notice who turns up and who doesn't. Just noticing can get in the way of an occupation of space. (Ahmed 2013)

Feminists have long contested citational practices that exclude women, indigenous peoples, and people of colour. They have also pointed to the prevalent tendency of framing even feminist works within a male intellectual tradition. So, for me, retaining these names was also a matter of acknowledging the scholarship of the research participants. But since research protocol disallows me from doing so, I have changed the names of the student participants, but tried my best to retain a sense of cultural identity and locational politics. The names of faculty members have also not been revealed in this chapter.

Disciplining Women's Studies

To decipher the impulse to *discipline* Women's Studies, it is necessary to understand the genealogy of the discipline in the Indian context. The role of the state in framing women's studies as a new field of study is indispensible. It is under the aegis of the University Grants Commission (UGC) that the field was institutionalised and granted the status of a discipline in the late 1980s (John 2008). However, the inception of women's studies was marked as an intervention, a perspective, rather than a discipline (Krishna Raj 1986; Lal and Kumar 2002). In her introduction to *Women's Studies in India: A Reader*, Mary E. John points out that women's studies started with a focus on research, which unlike teaching, 'did not require a direct confrontation with institutional and disciplinary structures' (2008: 10). As teaching remained marginal to the women's studies project until the 1990s, the earliest efforts in curricular development emphasised the need for more research. Research and teaching were also constituted as mutually exclusive and thus, John argues, 'education could recede from view' (ibid.). Interestingly, even in the first decade of the twenty-first century, John terms women's studies a 'problem field—that is to say, a field composed of issues and problems—rather than a discipline' (ibid.: 15). Further, she points to the peculiar nature of the field within the education system and argues that there has been 'very little engagement with the uniqueness of its formation—What other examples can one offer where an openly political and non-neutral field was provided a place within the education system?' (ibid.: 16). Simultaneously, she cautions against reading this as a sign of success and draws attention to the fact that there is an increasing tendency of centralisation and control by state agencies within women's studies.

One of the characteristics that Eloise Burker focuses on, in contemplating what constitutes a discipline, is 'a past, a present, and a future' that 'confer(s) identities on its practicing members' (2003: 74). Given the relative obscurity of the discipline, especially in non-metropolitan locations, students and research scholars I spoke to often articulated their participation in research as an act of writing this history into being.[7] Almost every research participant spoke about the lack of visibility of and knowledge about the discipline even within higher educational institutions. Consequently, this was linked to the poor status associated with the discipline even amongst the social sciences. The need to think, critique, and write about the discipline itself was impressed upon. And so, even as interdisciplinarity was thought of as a key feature of women's studies, its precarity within the higher education system encouraged the need to 'discipline' it, as it were. Surya,[8] a 28-year-old PhD candidate and a first-generation learner, highlighted the fact that those disciplinarily trained in women's studies often do not land jobs teaching the discipline. Not only do a limited number of universities offer the course, even those that do tend to hire people trained in other disciplines and who lack a political and theoretical perspective on gender. While acknowledging her love for women's studies and the ways in which it has enabled her growth as a person, Surya laments her chances at the academic job market. She suggests that introducing undergraduate programmes in women's studies may not only strengthen the discipline and inculcate a feminist perspective, but also ensure employability for those like her. She makes her case by calling attention to the fact that while there is a National Eligibility Test (NET) for lectureship in the subject, the State Eligibility Test (SET) is yet to include women's studies in the list of disciplines for which it conducts exams at the state level.

Recognition from the state and a trend towards vocationalisation were not simply negotiated with, but actively desired in these locations. Multiple conversations with Master's students and doctoral candidates from this location show that despite poor awareness about the discipline, most students initially decided, or in some cases were allowed by their families, to pursue this course because it would make them employable. Following from this, it can be argued that vocationalisation has encouraged the inclusion of students who have been traditionally disenfranchised from higher education due to their class and caste locations. The focus on finding a job, and consequently financial autonomy, is not seen as mutually exclusive to the performance of a feminist politics but, in fact, as a crucial factor enabling it.

Marking the centrality of interdisciplinarity in the formulation of women's studies, the UGC in 2012 defined it as 'a branch of study with a core area of theory, within an interdisciplinary framework that improves concepts from various social sciences, humanities and sciences' (*Twelfth Plan Guidelines* 2012: 10). However, many research participants expressed conflicting views regarding the interdisciplinarity of women's studies. While they approved the idea of the discipline looking at a variety of traditional disciplines (economics, sociology, health, law, etc.) through a gendered lens, thereby enabling an understanding of the relationality of macro-structures and intersectionality of oppressions, few research participants saw interdisciplinarity as beneficial in terms of methodological inputs or theoretical frameworks. This stemmed from a near-complete alienation from the disciplines in which they were formerly trained. A large number of students, uninterested faculty, and lack of bridge material to help the students comprehend the subject in a language they were comfortable in were listed as factors contributing to this alienation. The 'interdisciplinary' nature of women's studies is then perceived as a benefit simply because it allows for the movement of students away from these stifling disciplines and to be accepted into its fold a discipline more favourable to their pursuit of education. But the *interdisciplinary* character of women's studies is also often translated as *indiscipline*, which is seen as further lowering the status of the discipline. Rani, a 27-year-old research scholar who has completed her MA in women's studies and is currently working on a PhD that examines women's participation in water governance at the local level, offers one such perspective. She explains that while scholars from myriad disciplines are welcomed into the field, many tend to belittle the expertise of those trained in the discipline. Further, Rani points out that even scholars who may espouse deeply patriarchal politics get hired simply because they have worked on 'women' within their respective disciplines. Underscoring the long struggle that led to women's studies being institutionalised, she insists that those within the discipline should make the effort to persevere with the feminist principles that this discipline was built on. This, she feels, can happen only when both teachers and students work with a women's studies perspective.[9]

The research participants' anxiety to 'discipline' women's studies can be read as an attempt to address the precarity of the discipline and establish a scholarly identity for themselves within academia. This anxiety is equally a feature of metropolitan and non-metropolitan women's studies, as evinced by writing in both popular media (Ara 2020; Phadke 2017; Nair 2019), academic journals (Sharma 2017) and newsletters. It is, of course, fuelled by the challenges posed to the existence of the discipline by both neoliberal logic and right-wing ideology in the current moment (Phadke 2017). However, there are critical overlaps and disjunctures in the articulation of this anxiety. In metropolitan centres of women's studies, there is a growing focus on decolonising the discipline (Hussein and Hussain 2019), and a fear of a crisis in the discipline, fuelled by ideas of a politically motivated expansion causing a dip in 'standards', further delegitimising an already precarious discipline (Anandhi 2017). However, in the locations where this research is situated, what was more strongly articulated was the fear of non-acceptance of expertise. While the aim of the discipline is to democratise knowledge, the sharp conflict between the aspiration towards democratisation on the one hand, and an educational system that privileges exclusivity and equates it to excellence on the other, leads to a notion of instability. It is within this context that interdisciplinarity and precarity get enunciated as undesired indiscipline. This is only a preliminary exploration of these sentiments, and I suggest that it is important to reflect more on this as a way of gaining insight into the frames of reference that both define and delimit our understanding of women's studies as a discipline.

Disciplining is also achieved through the formation of strong national and regional networks of women's studies activism and academia. Both BDU and BU are members of the Indian Association for Women's Studies (IAWS) and the Regional Association for Women's Studies (RAWS). Not only faculty, but research students are also life members of these associations. Conferences and workshops organised by these bodies were thought of as opportunities to meet, debate, and learn with scholars from every part of the country. They were also seen as useful platforms to present work and receive feedback. Rani, a lifetime member of both RAWS and IAWS, has taken part in three IAWS conferences thus far. At one of these conferences, she presented a paper on sand mining in Karur district and the women's struggle to protect land resources. She fondly remembers being appreciated for her work. She also excitedly recounts to me her experience at the 2008 IAWS conference in Lucknow where she was overjoyed to find almost forty students enrolled in the women's studies programme at Lucknow University. That the discipline was not just recognised, but had good enrolment was, to her, a testament of its legitimacy. For Rani, these spaces catered not just to her academic aspirations but also served as affirmations of her professional and political choices.

The associations were also perceived as spaces where faculty members could converse about pedagogical practices and curriculum-building. Given the lack of textbooks in a young discipline such as women's studies, these groups were seen as instrumental in helping formulate a core syllabus that could be shared across centres. Faculty members highlighted the importance of publication of theses and research papers by the IAWS in light of the lack of local theoretical frameworks that are both relevant and accessible to students in the Indian context.

These organisations were also framed as collectives that could negotiate with the government in order to bring women's studies into the mainstream. A faculty member from BU asserts that RAWS and IAWS have represented stakeholders for a whole range of issues to the government—starting from including women's studies along with social work when the government calls for applications for certain positions. She remembers the time when a colleague from the discipline was unable to register with the employment exchange because there was no code for women's studies. She herself had registered under psychology because that was what her PhD was in.

Writing about the activities of the RAWS, N. Manimekalai (2017) lists their efforts in lobbying with the state for visibility and recognition, from inclusion of the discipline in state recruitment bodies to undertaking policy research in collaboration with WSCs across the state. In fact, members of this regional association played a key role as part of an IAWS delegation in urging the state to reconsider its fund cuts and non-release of grants after the end of the Twelfth Plan in 2017 (Manimekalai 2019). Even as the regional focus consolidates the position of the discipline vis-à-vis the state, and reiterates the expertise of scholars from non-metropolitan locations, it simultaneously opens up the possibility of a 'regional' critique of metropolitan women's studies, which seeks to make these locations 'colonies in the field of knowledge production' (Ramagorakh 2019: 29), identifies the uneven development of the discipline across regions

(Shankar 2019), and encourages a rethinking of the oft-repeated origin stories of the discipline allowing for a re-visioning of its future.

Decentring Women's Studies

In this section of the chapter, I suggest that the democratisation of the discipline is not just about *who* is able to access the discipline, but also *what* gets enunciated within the discipline. The inclusion of students from marginalised locations has, I argue, enabled a refashioning of the women's studies discourse in India. Historically, the metropolitan feminist has spoken about herself or her counterpart in non-metropolitan locations, usually *speaking for* her counterpart (John 1996; Niranjana 2010). By gaining access to institutional women's studies, the non-metropolitan feminist is able to speak for herself and her immediate community.

In elucidating their contribution to the larger women's studies *academe* in the country, the research participants spoke extensively about doing research rooted in their immediate contexts and the significance of these research projects. Topics that they worked on included intra-state migration of women involved in domestic labour, continued caste-based victimisation of the families of honour-killing victims, sexual and reproductive rights of disabled women, negotiations around sexual harassment within the university, challenges faced by mothers of disabled children, Toda women's socioeconomic conditions, and women's role in water governance in the region. All these projects were based in locations in Tiruchirappalli and Coimbatore districts. Nithyapriya, a Master's student in BU, contextualised her research on collectivisation of women labourers in the Valparai tea estates vis-à-vis her location. She told me about growing up with intimate knowledge of what it meant to work in one of these tea estates—both her parents are tea-plantation workers. Over the course of a year, she interviewed seventy labourers, spoke to them about how their health had been affected by chemicals used in the plantations, and how discrimination was experienced within this workplace. She was also interested in understanding their efforts to come together as a community and unionise in order to demand their rights.

The research participants invoked their positionality as 'outsider(s) within' to emphasise their contributions to the discipline of women's studies. This is not to position scholars from this location simply as 'area experts', but to acknowledge their production of *situated knowledges* which 'require that the object of knowledge be pictured as an actor and agent, not as a screen or a ground or a resource' (Haraway 1988).

The decentring of women's studies discourse is also enabled by making feminist discourse legible to communities outside the university. Women's Studies Centres at both BDU and BU are robustly involved in advocacy, extension activities, and skill development. Faculty at both centres believe that not only is this in accordance with the UGC guidelines for WSCs, it also provides their students necessary learning opportunities. Both centres conduct gender sensitisation workshops in the organised and unorganised sectors, with students, teachers, media professionals, government officials, self-help groups, link workers, and fieldworkers. They are also engaged in capacity-building training for academic managers, women entrepreneurs, and students, and train their students to be resource persons for gender sensitisation workshops. Discussing one of their most successful advocacy projects, the Menstrual Health Management (MHM) Programme, a faculty member from BDU highlights how research and advocacy feed into each other. The MHM programme has been functional since 2010 and was the outcome of departmental research which found that women continued to be reluctant to discuss menstrual health. This led to the formation of a forum to initiate conversations on women's reproductive health, particularly menstruation. The MHM programme, organised in association with the Tiruchirappalli Gynaecological Association, not only provided clinical support, but has also sought to publicly address social and cultural issues associated with menstruation. For instance, based on conversations with women, the students and the faculty have made an educational documentary called *Theetu*[10] about the social exclusion of women during the period of menstruation.

Research scholars at BDU working on the issue of health are also trained to function as MHM resource persons. They, in turn, address peers from affiliated colleges who are then expected to return to their respective colleges and engage with their colleagues. The scholars also conduct workshops in schools. There is thus an active encouragement of peer-to-peer advocacy and creation of resources in the local language. While there is an emphasis, no doubt, on the situatedness of their advocacy, crucial transnational links are also forged in the process. Women's studies scholars in these locations actively stake their claim to spaces within hegemonic English-language feminist discourse. They rue the difficulty in getting published in journals of 'international repute' due to their perceived lack of English language skills; nevertheless, there is a concerted effort to publish in English for the sake of reaching a wider audience and being acknowledged within the mainstream feminist academic discourse. Students and faculty often publish in IAWS newsletters and collections and in turn access these sources for their own work. They also insert themselves in transnational circuits of feminist discourse by getting involved in research funded by State agencies like the UGC and the Indian Council of Social Science Research (ICSSR), as well as international organisations such as the United Nations Children's Fund (UNICEF), United Nations Development Programme (UNDP), Ford Foundation, World Health Organization (WHO), etc. While S. Anandhi frames such research as 'merely validat(e)ing the state project of women's empowerment with no interrogation of research methods and practices of different disciplines' (2017: 62), participants in this research viewed them as attempts to broker mobility of not just students, who often aspire to move to metropolises both in India and abroad for further studies, but also of particular 'regional' discourses.

In recognising that the question of gender has, in Tamil Nadu, been long-debated within the anti-caste and labour movements, these centres have since their inception included thinkers and philosophers like Iyothee Thass, an anti-caste Tamil scholar who encouraged conversion to Buddhism as early as 1898, and Periyar E. V. Ramasami, founder of the Self Respect movement, in their syllabi, thereby questioning the usual rendering of the social reform and nationalist movements as the origin story[11] of the contemporary women's movement in the country. Rather than assuming that these regional narratives lie outside the national, such narratives prompt a reconsideration of the complex ways in which multiple narratives interact with each other. These are not simply regional retellings of the genealogy of the women's studies movement in the country, but as S. Sreekumar (2017) argues, these linkages provide us with the necessary tools to work through some of the impasses that confront the discipline and its politics in the current moment. The multiplicity of histories allows us to reconsider our present, and re-envision our futures within the discipline.

Discussing the potential for dissent within women's studies, in the context of state funding and work on government projects, Kalairani, a Master's student at BHU who hails from Kammampatti in Salem district, drew a parallel between the women's movement and the discipline of women's studies. She said that just like the movement's negotiations with the State to bring about legislative change do not take away from its subversive potential, projects undertaken by WSCs with government funding can and do retain their oppositional value despite working on goals as envisioned by the UGC's five-year plan.

Mary E. John suggests that 'the Indian state has been the [women's] movement's most constitutive site of contestation' (1996: 3073) before pointing out the many instances where the women's movement has deployed the rhetoric of nationalism and development in order to negotiate with the State. The concept note for the Sixteenth National Conference on Women's Studies (2020) organised by the IAWS notes how the movement's continued engagement with notions of constitutional rights have resulted in law and policy changes (*IAWS Newsletter* 2019). Thus, in calling upon the history and legacy of the women's movement, Kalairani not only defends non-metropolitan scholarship and activism, but also successfully inserts them into a mainstream narrative of the national movement, thus staking claim to both legitimacy and recognition.

Pedagogies that include local language texts—not just essays, but also Tamil fiction and poetry—are a feature in both universities (Kanagasabai 2020), as is peer learning. Peer learning becomes a strategy to deal with limited financial, and therefore limited pedagogic resources within the departments (Kanagasabai 2018). This is not to gloss over structural inequities, but to recognise that the 'political' needs to be defined in relation to its wider context. For instance, Surya spoke at length about the gender study circle that students of BDU facilitate within university premises. Students from various departments invested in discussing and understanding the social implications of gender meet every Wednesday. The group decides on a topic to be discussed and the readings are sent out in advance. An independent student-run initiative, this study circle also self-published a few issues of a journal they named *Thedal.*[12] While lack of resources spelt an end to the journal's run, the robust discussions in the study circle continue.

Thus the students and scholars at BDU and BU saw themselves as contributing to the discipline of women's studies by networking with a wide spectrum of people engaged in teaching, training, advocacy, capacity-building, field action projects, and research. They perceived knowledge-making and theory-building to be situated practices, and were involved in collaborative pedagogical practices. As much as the 'local' was emphasised in their research, they saw their work in relation to national and transnational movements, activism, and research. Acknowledging the problems inherent in an educational system with Brahminical hegemony, Anglophone supremacy, and state-controlled agendas, they recognised the subversive potential afforded by this new discipline, itself at the margins of the academic institution, and its intersectional approach. Through their scholarship and activism, they not only enable their own transformations, but also transform the disciplinary boundaries and practices of women's studies.

Following from this, I suggest that women's studies scholars in non-metropolitan locations are enabling a decentring of feminist discourse in a quest for cognitive justice. Indian sociologist Shiv Visvanathan (2009) proposes that

> cognitive justice recognises the right of different forms of knowledge to co-exist, but adds that this plurality needs to go beyond tolerance or liberalism to an active recognition for the need of diversity. It

> demands recognition of knowledges, not only as methods but as ways of life.

Foregrounding the lived experiences of women's studies scholars in these locations was not simply aimed at resisting or rupturing the dominant narrative of women's studies that is produced in metropolitan circuits; rather, it is the production of a different, partial narrative that can contest the dominant and minimise its violence.

Concluding Notes

I began this chapter with the premise that a critical examination of the experiences and situated knowledge of those engaged in women's studies in non-metropolitan locations can open up the discussion on the status of the institutionalised discipline in the country. Engaging with the prevalent discourse of depoliticisation, NGOisation, and professionalisation of women's studies, I proposed the need to engage with the everyday experiences and perspectival knowledge of students and scholars from these locations in order to be attentive to the possibilities activated by non-metropolitan women's studies. As an institutionalised discipline, women's studies is still largely dependent on the State both for funding and for defining its mandate. Therefore, what I argue for is not a blindsiding of this fact, but a shift in the vantage point from macro-structures to micro-negotiations, to allow for a re-reading of a situation replete with discrepancies.

Despite prevalent anxieties about women's studies losing its radical edge, I argue that its perceived location at the margins of established academia, combined with its precarity, make it a curious but potent site for oppositional academic activity. I posit that it is the precarity of the discipline that also strengthens the impulse to 'discipline' women's studies, make it a boundaried system, and inculcate gatekeeping practices. Highlighting the negotiations involved in pedagogical practice, examining not just who speaks but what gets enunciated and who is allowed to be part of a feminist community, this chapter locates decentring as a feminist act. It situates women's studies scholars in these locations as academics who struggle both *within* and *against* institutions of power. In complicating the desire to belong and yet challenge the established practices of recognition of expertise, the chapter indicates the ways in which non-metropolitan women's studies allows for a reimagination of its academic project.

Finally, in discussing the twin impulses of disciplining and decentring, this chapter posits *indiscipline* as a desirable way of being and becoming within women's studies. However, rather than advocating a simplistic removal of administrative categories in favour of a utopic synthesis of disciplines, this is a call to actively participate in a continual and essential re-examination of how, by whom, and under what auspices knowledge is produced within *academe*. In doing so, one hopes for a mutual learning of alternative imagination, one which can hold space for contending imaginaries and diverse perspectives—*indiscipline*—within the academic discipline of women's studies.

Notes

1. I would like to thank the students and faculty members of the WSCs at Bharathidasan University, Tiruchirappalli and Bharathiar University, Coimbatore. They welcomed me into their universities, their classrooms, their discussions, their homes, and were ever willing to engage. I would also like to thank Dr Asha Achuthan and Dr Shilpa Phadke for their thoughtful and constructive feedback on this chapter.
2. For a detailed discussion on the regional and social contexts of these students, see Kanagasabai (2018).
3. S. Anandhi (2017) points out that the state of Tamil Nadu has the highest number of private and self-financed colleges.
4. While John (2017) notes the democratisation of higher education in general, I have later in the chapter argued that the expansion of the women's studies project in particular has allowed for the democratisation of the discipline.
5. At the beginning of the Tenth Plan Period (2002–2007) there were thirty-four WSCs across the country (of which thirteen were created in the Ninth Plan Period). As of 2018, there were 163 WSCs, of which several are located in smaller cities and towns in the country. However, the expiry of the Twelfth Plan (2012–2017) and continuing uncertainty over funding for the existing centres have adversely impacted further expansion of the institutionalised discipline.

6. The Centre for Women's Studies was established in Bharathiar University in December 2004 and in Bharathidasan University in 2005.

7. As I have argued elsewhere,

> Experiential modes, even if employed, are restricted to discourse about the discipline from the point of view of the pedagogue. The changing demography of the students of Women's Studies, their self-perceptions and their locations within circuits of feminist epistemology do not find space for articulation. (Kanagasabai 2018: 710)

8. All names used for student research participants are pseudonyms.

9. The term 'women's studies perspective' is preferred over 'feminism' as the latter is linked to 'certain imagined standards and competency' and thus perceived as unsuitable to their own identification. For more on this, see Kanagasabai (2018).

10. Tamil word which refers to a practice of segregation based on a notion of ritual pollution.

11. See John (2008); Krishna Raj (1986); Lal and Kumar (2002); and Sreekumar (2017).

12. Tamil word that can be roughly translated as the act of seeking or searching.

References

Ahmed, S. 2013. 'Making Feminist Points'. *Feminist Killjoys*, 11 September. Available at http://feministkilljoys.com/2013/09/11/making-feminist-points/ (accessed November 2023).

Anandhi, S. 2017. 'Women's Studies in Tamil Nadu: A Curious Case of Institutionalization'. *Women in a Changing World: Restructured Inequalities, Countercurrents and Sites of Resistance* (Proceedings of the XV National Conference on Women's Studies): 60–63. Chennai: Indian Association for Women's Studies.

Anandhi, S., and P. Swaminathan. 2006. 'Making it Relevant: Mapping the Meaning of Women's Studies in Tamil Nadu'. *Economic and Political Weekly* 41 (42): 4444–4454.

Ara, I. 2020. 'As Students and Teachers Panic, Jamia Withdraws Notice Disbanding Two Departments.' *The Wire*, 7 April. Available at https://thewire.in/education/as-students-and-teachers-panic-jamia-withdraws-notice-disbanding-two-departments (accessed November 2023).

Burker, E. 2003. 'Is Women's Studies a Disciplinary or an Interdisciplinary Field of Inquiry?' *National Women's Studies Association (NWSA) Journal* 15 (1): 73–93.

Haraway, D. 1988. 'Situated Knowledges: The Science Question in Feminism and the Privilege of Partial Perspective'. *Feminist Studies* 14 (3): 575–599.

Hussein, N., and S. Hussain. 2019. 'Decolonising Gender in South Asia: A Border Thinking Perspective'. *Third World Thematics* 4 (4–5): 261–270.

IAWS Newsletter. 2019. 'Constitutional Principles in 21st Century India: Visions for Emancipation'. XVI National Conference on Women's Studies. Volume 4 (3): 3–4.

John, M. E. 1996. 'Gender and Development in India, 1970s–1990s: Some Reflections on the Constitutive Role of Contexts'. *Economic and Political Weekly* 31 (47): 3071–3077.

______. 2008. 'Introduction'. In *Women's Studies in India: A Reader*: 1–19. New Delhi: Penguin Books.

______. 2017. 'Gender, Sexual Harassment and the Democratization of Higher Education Today'. *Women in a Changing World: Restructured Inequalities, Countercurrents and Sites of Resistance* (Proceedings of the XV National Conference on Women's Studies): 67–69. Chennai: Indian Association for Women's Studies.

Kanagasabai, N. 2018. 'Possibilities of Transformation: Women's Studies in Tier II Cities in Tamil Nadu, India'. *Discourse: Studies in the Cultural Politics of Education* 39 (5): 709–722.

______. 2020. 'Language, Little Magazines, and Local Feminisms'. In *The Handbook of Magazine Studies*, M. Sternadori and T. Holmes (eds): 333–341. New Jersey: John Wiley & Sons, Inc.

Krishna Raj, M. (eds). 1986. *Women's Studies in India: Some Perspectives*. Bombay: Popular Prakashan.

Lal, M., and S. P. Kumar (eds). 2002. *Women's Studies in India*. Shimla: Institute of Advanced Studies.

Manimekalai, N. 2017. 'Women's Studies in Tamil Nadu: A Journey Replete with Challenges'. *XV National Conference of Women's Studies*: 56–60. Chennai: Indian Association of Women's Studies.

______. 2019. 'IAWS and UGC Women's Studies Centres: Solidarity and Collective Action'. *IAWS Newsletter* (November): 38–40.

Nair, A. 2019. 'Members of Women's Studies Centres Upset with Major Cuts in UGC Funds'. *The Times of India*, 19 March. Available at https://timesofindia.indiatimes.com/city/pune/members-of-womens-studies-centres-upset-with-major-cuts-in-ugc-funds/articleshow/68475874.cms (accessed November 2023).

Niranjana, T. 2010. 'Why Culture Matters: Rethinking the Language of Feminist Politics'. *Inter-Asia Cultural Studies* 11 (2): 229–235.

Phadke, S. 2017. 'Why is the Government Threatened by Women's Studies Centres in Indian Universities?' *The Indian Express*, 15 June. Available at https://indianexpress.com/article/education/why-is-the-government-threatened-by-womens-studies-centres-in-indian-universities/ (accessed November 2023).

Ramagorakh, D. 2019. 'Status of Women's Studies in Vidarbha (Maharashtra): The UGC Neither Allows Them to Beg, Nor Do The Universities Allow Them to Live'. *IAWS Newsletter* (November): 28–30.

Roy, S. 2009. 'Melancholic Politics and the Politics of Melancholia: The Indian Women's Movement'. *Feminist Theory* 10 (3): 341–357.

Shankar, S. 2019. 'The Jharkhand Project: Towards Developing Women's Studies in Jharkhand'. *IAWS Newsletter* (November): 31–32.

Sharma, A. 2017. 'Why Women's Studies? Contemporary Relevance and Future Discourse'. *Economic and Political Weekly* 52 (21). Available at https://epw.in/journal/2017/21/web-exclusives/why-womens-studies.html (accessed November 2023).

Sreekumar, S. 2017. 'Equivocations of Gender: Feminist Storytelling and Women's Studies in the Contemporary'. *Indian Journal of Gender Studies*: 24 (1): 47–68.

Twelfth Plan Guidelines (2012–2017). 2012. University Grants Commission. Available at https://www.ugc.ac.in/pdfnews/8004557_WS-Guidelines_XII-Plan_Revised-Final.pdf (accessed November 2023).

Visvanathan, S. 2009. 'The Search for Cognitive Justice'. *Seminar* 597 (May).

Part III

Ruptures or Repetitions?

6 Westernising Feminist Futures
Women's and Gender Studies in the Age of Terror

Sunera Thobani

Introduction

The 'War on Terror' has had a deeply transformative effect on Western societies, particularly with regard to gender and sexual politics. As I demonstrate in this chapter, the theoretical interventions of renowned feminist intellectuals during the early phase of the war grounded this conflict in the terrain of gender politics. By analysing a number of feminist theoretical interventions vis-à-vis the development of women's and gender studies in the West, I argue that these feminist interventions contributed to the ideology of the war on terror and served to advance the imperialist interests of Western nation-States.

The history of women's and gender studies as an academic field in the West is generally traced to second wave feminism, which originated in North America and Europe during the 1960s and 1970s. The feminist activism of this period is generally defined as centred on women's access to abortion rights, sexual freedom, violence against women, and equality in education, employment, and political participation. In tandem with the political activism of this movement, feminist activists located in the university began to develop and offer courses on women's history, inequalities, employment, and related issues, which were integrally connected to the feminist consciousness-raising groups and women's anti-violence organisations budding across the Western world—so goes the narrative within the discipline.

Eventually, these developments led to the founding of programmes, and later departments, of women's and gender studies, with their related professional associations and research and publication networks.

Within this new interdisciplinary field and the feminist theories that grounded it, a singular focus on 'Woman' as a universal category elevated gender to a position of primacy and reified patriarchy as a cross-historical and transcultural phenomenon that was responsible for the global oppression of women (see, for example, the foundational texts of the field by Gayle Rubin, Susan Brownmiller, Mary Daly, Phyllis Chesler, Betty Friedan, Andrea Dworkin, Shulamith Firestone, Kate Millett, Gloria Steinem, Catharine MacKinnon, and Adrienne Rich). The remit of women's and gender studies soon expanded to include the study of class as feminists from the political left challenged the liberalism that had dominated the earlier feminist project (Maria Mies, Margaret Benston, Zillah Eisenstein, etc.). Feminist theoretical and political traditions were at the time generally grouped into liberal, socialist, and radical feminisms, this approach being dominant within women's and gender studies courses through the 1980s and well into the 1990s. The curriculum quickly expanded to include the study of women in economy, law, and family, as well as in medicine, science, and technology. The odd 'Global Feminism' or 'Black Women's History' course was offered in these programmes—these stood in for the issues of women from across the non-Western world in the more internationally-minded feminist departments. For the most part, however, the three trajectories of Western feminist theory set the theoretical and political parameters of the field. The centring of gender within all three drew attention not only to the forms of oppression and exploitation that shaped the lives of women, but also demonstrated how the social world itself was gendered.

The impact of these developments on established disciplines was profound. The growing visibility of feminist theory and gender studies led the dominant disciplines to integrate the study of women and gender into their respective areas of study. Since those early heady days, women's and gender studies has expanded to become more inclusive of 'difference' as the concerns of women of colour, indigenous women, and women from the Third World became more visible. The narrative of 'inclusion' is now entrenched in the field.

Moreover, the institutionalisation and mainstreaming of women's and gender studies during this period brought it closer to the centres of power—that is, to the State across the West and much of the Global South (through various commissions and inquiries into the 'Status of Women', its ministries and secretaries of State, and welfare programmes); the academy (including departments and programmes, extension of gender-based curricula, and gender equity-focused administration, etc.); the media (feminist media and cultural production); and the economy (employment and pay equity, maternity benefits, etc, in the public sector as well as the corporate world).

Yet the field itself was contested from its very beginnings, both for its foundational gesture of universalising the category 'Woman' and for its race-blind approach, which implicitly centred the Whiteness of its founders as normative to the feminist project. Even as the field was being institutionalised, anti-racist and anti-colonial feminist theory and action—including discourses pioneered by Black and indigenous women, women from the Third World, and women of colour—gained considerable ground in the political, cultural, and intellectual arenas. Feminists within these traditions contested the epistemological authority, privileged position, and power of Western feminism and its power to define feminist politics and projects (Amos and Parmar 1984; Davis 1983; Torres, Mohanty and Russo 1991).

In the US and Canada, indigenous women challenged the genocidal practices of the settler colonial nation-State, including the ongoing dispossession of their territories, which had particularly gendered consequences. Specific State policies directly targeted women who, given their powerful positions in pre-colonial matrilineal and matriarchal indigenous societies, were being systematically disenfranchised (LaDuke 1997; Maracle 1988; Monture Angus 1995). In the US, Angela Davis (1983) studied the historical role of White women in organising and maintaining the system of plantation slavery, highlighting the ways in which they facilitated the racial/sexual violence experienced by Black women. She also drew attention to the racism of the early White suffragists, who actively opposed citizenship rights for Black men at a time when Black communities were being terrorised by White supremacist groups, including the Klu Klux Klan (ibid.). Cheryl Harris (1993) followed with her groundbreaking essay that reconceptualised Whiteness as not just an identity, but a form of property that has been historically protected within US law. Tracing how slavery continues to organise contemporary social relations, Harris demonstrated that Whiteness as property endows those who embody it with valuable forms of citizenship, rights, and belonging that are denied to Black people, women as well as men. Such a racial distribution of rights and entitlements, Harris demonstrated, is routinely upheld in court practice that 'extends to whites' settled expectations of continued privilege' (Harris 1993: 1758).

Anti-racist critiques forwarded by women of colour during this period also contested the border control policies of State and nation, as well as the racialisation of national subjects through immigration, citizenship rights, and social forms of belonging (Bannerji 1995; Lowe 1996). Focusing on the politics of language, representation, and state practices, these critiques were greatly enhanced by the development of the concept of intersectionality within the Black feminist tradition (Crenshaw 1991; see also Hill Collins 1990). My brief outline of these developments should not be taken as a suggestion that a particular symmetry of experience or common structural location characterised the relationships amongst the various communities represented within the anti-racist and anti-colonial traditions referenced above. Indeed, the asymmetrical relations of power within and between these communities, which reflect racial hierarchies that operate at the global level, run deep and even now derail projects of political solidarity and coalitional politics. The key point is that these feminist and womanist traditions all rejected the elevation of gender as primary in the organisation of the social order by taking into account the racial/colonial/sexual relations that are the bedrock of North American society, and indeed, Western society and the international order more generally.

In the UK, for example, Valerie Amos and Pratibha Parmar described as 'imperial feminism' the installation of a 'particular tradition, Eurocentric and western... as the only legitimate feminism in current political practice' (1984: 44). Critiquing the feminist concept of *herstory*, 'which white women use to trace the roots of women's oppression or to justify some form of political practice' (ibid.: 46), Amos and Parmar demonstrated how this elides the colonial, neo-colonial and imperial relations that shape the history being reclaimed for women by feminists. The concept of herstory, they concluded, 'suffers the same form of historical amnesia of white male historians' (ibid.: 46). The growth of Black feminism since the mid-1970s, they further argued, 'has forced the question of the centrality of Black women's oppression onto the political and theoretical agendas' (ibid.: 44). Highlighting the grassroots activism of Black women (a category which then included women of African and Asian descent in the context of the UK) that contested the power of the British state and its racist policies, Amos and Parmar argued that White women's feminism—and the concepts they had developed—was not only oppressive to Black women but led to very tangible benefits for White women. Critique of the exoticisation of Asian and Black women in UK feminist campaigns against 'dowry deaths', 'arranged marriages', 'female genital mutilation', etc., and their fusing with the racist immigrant policies of the State, were key concerns of these anti-racist politics. Similarly, Chandra Mohanty's (Torres, Mohanty, and Russo 1991) analysis of the construction of the 'third world woman' within the sub-field of feminist development studies showed how this monolithic image of a uniformly powerless and oppressed victim enabled Western feminists to constitute their own subjectivity as the agents of emancipation. In short, the politics and movements discussed above rejected the power of Western feminisms to speak in the name of all women by debunking its foundational idea of universal 'womanhood'.

In the 1990s, the concept of intersectionality was developed within Black feminist theory; this soon became a major theoretical innovation in advancing anti-racist critiques of hegemonic feminism. In her groundbreaking essay on violence against women of colour in the US, legal scholar Kimberley Crenshaw (1991) mounted a defence of identity politics to argue that identity *matters*, given that the violence experienced by women of colour is shaped as much by racial identity, class, and sexuality as it is by their gender. Indeed, as Crenshaw went on to demonstrate in her study of immigration and anti-domestic violence laws, the policies of rape crisis centres that centred the White, middle-class woman effectively barred women of colour from accessing the network of anti-violence services developed by feminist organisations. While identity-based political struggles could have the effect of obscuring internal hierarchies within particular communities, intersectional approaches would effectively highlight the impact of such asymmetries of power on women (ibid.). The centring of race, class, and sexuality in the construction of gender—fundamental to the concept of intersectionality—became a milestone, and its popularity across women of colour feminisms led to a flourishing of anti-racist studies and political solidarities. Intersectionality as conceptualised here was not an amalgamation of an abstracted assortment of reified identities or social divides, but rather a carefully delineated study of the entangled social relations that organise the material and sociocultural world, highlighting the crucial place of race in this matrix.

These complex and richly layered traditions, while countering the hegemony of Western feminism, also laid bare its complicity with colonialism, racism, and imperialism. However, these critiques were met with either silence or token inclusion. In Canada, mainstream feminists adopted multicultural policies of racial management—strategies developed by the State—in their own interactions with, and accommodation of, the political movements of women of colour. Women's and gender studies, like mainstream feminist organisations, began to include a token woman of colour or two into their programmes and increased course offerings on 'global feminism', 'third world feminisms' or other variations on such homogenising themes and approaches, which ultimately reproduced the older racial/colonial discourses. However, the internal challenges by women of colour to Western feminism were growing in intensity and scale and emerged as a destabilising force. By the 1990s, a backlash was developing within women's and gender studies: there arose a tendency to elevate a strand of sexuality politics defined not in relation, but in opposition to the anti-racist politics of women of colour, even though queer academics/activists of colour had been instrumental in shaping the course of sexuality politics. The elevation of this White-identified sexuality politics (Smith 2010; Thobani 2022) led to a further displacement of race and coloniality from the conceptual field. Intersectionality was appropriated to focus solely on sexuality, while marginalising the question of race and coloniality.

The gender/sexual/racial politics I am mapping out here took a dramatic turn following '9/11' (as the 11 September 2001 attack on the World Trade Centre, New York came to be known) and the launch of the US-led 'War on Terror'. The George W. Bush administration identified the elimination of 'terrorists' and the 'liberation' of Afghan women as key foreign policy objectives, making gender a key consideration in the global war.[1] The US response to the 9/11 attacks thus reframed them from a confrontation with its foreign policy in the Middle East and Central Asia to an all-out attack by 'Islamic terror' and Muslim men on human civilisation, conflating the West with humanity in the process. In this reframing, Islam was constructed as inherently implicated in fanaticism as well as misogyny. As other Western nation-States fell in line with the US position, news media and popular culture across North America and Europe became quickly saturated with images of veiled Muslim women, now symbolising the 'Islamic' hatred of women. As I have discussed elsewhere, the images of veiled women were accompanied with those of bearded and armed Muslim men, or with images of Islam's sacred text, the Qur'an (Thobani 2007). The conflation of Islam, terrorism, and misogyny that permeated these constructs gendered and racialised the discourse of terror and mobilised public support for the invasion of Afghanistan as a feminist cause, that is, as a means to 'save' Muslim women. The manner in which feminist activists and scholars in the West took up the war on terror in their intellectual, cultural, and political work, and the transformative impact of such engagement on women's and gender studies is analysed in the following section.

Feminist and Gender/Sexual Politics in the Global War

Feminist engagement with the global war on terror is significant as it has not only transformed feminist politics in the West but also reshaped the field of women's and gender studies. While the Islamophobic construct of Muslim women as objects of oppression has been contested by anti-racist and Muslim feminists (Arat-Koc 2002; Barlas 2002; Thobani 2002), virtually no attention has been paid to what the feminist debates about the 'real' nature of Islam and the 'real' relation of Muslim women to this tradition has accomplished *for* feminism, and for the field of women's and gender studies.

In an early paper, I had identified three main trends that emerged in hegemonic feminist responses to the Afghan war.[2] I tracked these trends in terms of the emergence of a number of novel theoretical advances as well as in the reworking of some older formulations, which I thematically grouped into the following: anti-Semitism; precariousness; and gender apartheid (Thobani 2007, 2010). I revisit these developments and also present a reading of a more recent crop of feminist texts to delineate the discursive practices they deploy. As my earlier study had demonstrated, these practices produce the figure of the Muslim as the gendered bearer of an absolute and deadly alterity in relation to the White gendered/sexual subject, with the latter defined as the 'real' target of 'Islamic terror'. My reading of the newer texts demonstrates how this White gendered/sexual subject is situated at the forefront of the Western epistemological tradition and defined as emblematic of its highest values.

The Gender of War

The feminist response to the war on terror was to mobilise public support in explicitly gendered terms. Although there exists a long tradition of western feminist critique of war as a masculine phenomenon, here the US-led invasion and occupation of Afghanistan was represented, in line with State rhetoric, primarily as the means to 'save' Afghan women and girls from misogynistic Muslim men. Gender equality was here naturalised as an integral value of Western culture, which made a gendered iteration of the 'White woman's burden' the dominant ethos of this political impetus to save 'the Muslim woman'.

This position was articulated most clearly in liberal feminist terms, particularly by feminists most closely associated with establishment politics. These feminists enthusiastically embraced the binary that shaped the Islamophobic discourse of the war—that of a civilised West valiantly confronting a terrorist Islam—allowing them to carve out a public space as expert commentators on the 'real' status of the Muslim woman. Such feminist expertise pivoted on the construction of the Muslim male as a hate-filled gender fanatic, and of the Muslim woman as either pathetic victim or willing dupe of the 'terrorist'. Islam, according to these feminists, promoted and sanctioned all manner of medieval barbarisms which were gendered in nature; Islam was thus a particular threat to woman—not only the Muslim woman 'imprisoned' in her veil, but also the Western woman, who was particularly vulnerable given her feminist commitments (Arat-Koc 2002: 433–444).[3] In elevating gender as a primary factor shaping international relations, this feminist approach, fixated on the veil, grounded the war's imperialist ideology within feminist politics. The 'clash of civilisations' was thus repositioned as really a 'clash of genders', feminist/Western progressivism versus medieval patriarchy; in the process, gender equality was redefined as a key cultural value of the West and hence irrefutable proof of its superiority (see for example, Armstrong 2003; Chesler 2003). The gender 'equality' being claimed here as cultural property of the West was its neoliberal, bourgeois variant, now enmeshed with imperialism and a war of occupation. The veil was a central trope in this feminist discourse as it signified not only the 'cultural barbarism' of Islam but also the 'cultural superiority' of the West.

Yet the veil also came to symbolise the duplicity of the Muslim woman in the work of some feminists who supported the war and advocated its expansion. Here, the Muslim woman, when not conceived of as a passive victim, was constructed as a murderous threat. One feminist who stood out early amongst these establishment feminists, and whose work remains considerably influential, was Phyllis Chesler, a psychologist and feminist activist, a founding figure of second wave feminism who is even now referred to as a 'Feminist Prophet'. Chesler's book on the global war, *The New Anti-Semitism* (2003), called for a total war led by the US and Israel on the entire Middle East and Central Asia. Well known for her Zionist politics and strong support of Israel, Chesler identified the US and Israel as twin targets of a terrorism which, she argued, was rooted in a 'new anti-Semitism', a singular threat to the West that emanated from Muslims, and in particular from Palestinians.

Redefining the 'West' as shaped by the Judeo-Christian tradition, and anti-Semitism to be 'as old as the Jews', Chesler's argument about the 'new' anti-Semitism was predicated on the idea of a contemporary religious and racial alliance between Christians and Jews. Muslims, in this view, were characterised by 'their' age-old enmity with both Jews and Christians. A strengthening of the alliance between the US (redefined as Christian in essence) with Israel (defined as Jewish, in essence) in a war on Muslims was thus necessary to protect the West. Furthermore, she argued, the Palestinians were a particularly pernicious enemy of this West, and the Palestinian woman, represented primarily as suicide bomber, was identified by Chesler as the deadly symbol of this enmity. She thus located the issue of Palestine at the centre of the Islamophobic ideology of the global war, and in a fit of racial/colonial paranoia, defined Israel, a settler-colonial society, as a victim of Palestinian violence, that is, of the very people the Israeli nation-State had colonised. With regard to the US, Chesler equated anti-racist feminist activism with victimising 'real' feminists. She condemned as 'faux' feminists those activists she identified as 'more concerned with racism than sexism', considering herself to have been victimised by them for her supposedly 'true' feminism.

It is interesting that Chesler uses her own experience (in her twenties, she married an Afghan man and moved to live with his family in Afghanistan) to describe the Islamic world as a state of 'imprisonment' for woman. In Afghanistan, as Chesler describes it, she witnessed a 'barbaric' form of 'gender apartheid' which included 'polygamy, purdah, women in burqas who were forced to sit at the back of the bus, arranged first-cousin marriages, child brides, honour killings' (Perry 2019). This particular representation of Muslim women and men, much like that of other 'Orientals', is, of course, littered throughout the colonial archive; the war on terror became the occasion for a feminist retrieval and circulation of the same. An interesting double move takes place in Chesler's narrative. She locates herself in the position of 'the' Muslim woman in her description of 'imprisonment' by her husband's family, yet also situates herself beyond this position for, unlike the Muslim woman, she recognises this to be a violation of her sense of self. What is absent in her discussion of life with this Afghan family is how her Whiteness, her status as an American woman, might have informed their treatment of her.

A number of feminists, including the feminist philosopher Judith Butler, spoke out against the policies of the Israeli State in the global war. However, the significance of Chesler's perspective lies in the ideological convergence of (liberal) feminist politics with Zionist and evangelical constituencies, which would eventually lead to the dominance of the far-right political factions in the US. While the idea of a religious bond between Israel and the US had earlier consolidated the support of the evangelical Christian right wing for the extremist Zionist lobby in the US, Chesler's work popularised and extended these views within feminist politics, and amongst women more generally, by grounding them in her feminist framework. Moreover, Chesler's redefinition of Western culture as 'Judeo-Christian' recast both as proto-feminist by suggesting that gender egalitarianism was at stake in both the Israeli occupation of Palestine and in the US invasion of Afghanistan.

The concept of the 'new anti-Semitism' has since become institutionalised in the US and Canada and is regularly used to clamp down on pro-Palestinian activism, particularly in the case of the Boycott, Divestment, and Sanctions (BDS) movement initiated by Palestinian civil society. This construct of anti-Semitism is deployed to claim that diasporic Muslim communities are irredeemably anti-Jewish, hate-filled, and violent.

Not surprisingly, Chesler supported a total ban on the burqa, arguing, 'The fact is that Muslim women are increasingly not given a free choice about wearing the veil, and those who resist are beaten, threatened with death, arrested, flogged, jailed, or murdered for honor by their own families, by vigilante groups, or by the state' (2010: 38). Noting in the most sensational, Orientalising manner that the veil does not protect Muslim women from harassment, rape, or stalking, she characterised Muslim men as engaged in various forms of violence against these women, including battery, forced marriage of very young girls to very old men, and daily beatings (ibid.). In supporting the ban, Chesler presented these forms of misogynist violence as the condition of everyday life for all Muslim women; like others in the West, she links the burqa to their sexuality and more directly, to their sexual brutalisation. This oppression of Muslim women and girls is presented as solely 'caused' by Islam and Islamic culture, and as having nothing to do with capitalist globalisation, imperialism, occupation, and neoliberalism (which have deepened violence and poverty across the Global South, with women and children bearing the brunt). Moreover, implicit in Chesler's account is the assumption that Western women are not beaten, stalked, raped, or murdered by their husbands and partners, that these women's lives are free of violence *only* because they are unveiled. Even as Chesler continues to voice her deeply racist and Islamophobic views, she is celebrated as a feminist icon for her 'remarkable contribution' that has 'saved women's lives and sanity', and for living 'A Life on Behalf of Women'; in the feminist circles associated with the network 'Women and Therapy', she is identified as a 'radical visionary' and 'feminist therapy pioneer' (Pitts 2017). The burqa has now been banned in public spaces in Austria, France, Canada (Quebec), Belgium, Germany (partial ban), and Bulgaria, with Denmark, Norway, and the Netherlands reportedly considering this possibility (Stack 2017). Feminists have not only done little to contest such racial targeting of Muslim women in these countries, they have actively supported the ban.

The feminist campaign to ban the burqa has not lost steam. It effectively prohibits Muslim women who wear the veil from accessing public services and hence reduces their access to education, health and social services, and in some cases, even to public transport. The ban also bars employment for veiled women in the public sector, significantly limiting their access to well-paid jobs. Such a move imposes a *de facto* (non)citizen status on these women and their families by excluding them from public spaces and institutions;[4] anecdotal accounts suggest that the ban has also encouraged out-migration of Muslim families from Europe and within Canadian provinces (see CBC News 2019; Nicolas 2022). It should be noted that in Canada, the province of Quebec, which enacted the ban, is generally considered the most progressive and left-leaning province in the country. In the case of France, Joan Scott (2007) has noted the very small numbers of Muslim women who wear the burqa; she argues that the fixation with the veil actually 'creates' the idea of the clash of civilisations by depicting the French nation as homogenous and unified in its outrage at the Muslim presence in that country.

The element of fantasy that drives the feminist position on the burqa cannot be overlooked:

> A burqa wearer may feel she cannot breathe, that she might slowly be suffocating. She may feel buried alive and may become anxious and or claustrophobic. Just imagine the consequences of getting used to this as a way of life.... The sight of women in burqas can be demoralizing and frightening to Westerners of all faiths, including Muslims, and not to mention secularists. (Chesler 2010)

Chesler, of course, is not alone in making the feminist case against the burqa during the global war—she has been joined by other feminists, including some Muslim activists, in condemning Islam, and vociferously criticising Muslim women. The trope of the burqa as a prison, a tomb, and a signifier of living death runs throughout the work of these feminists, whose self-presentation as 'authentic' insiders to Islam endows their work with greater force. In the context of the global war, such anti-Islam racism from Muslim feminists-as-native informants has allowed them access to upward social and professional mobility otherwise denied by the racial relations of power in Western societies. For example, here are the views of Irshad Manji, a Muslim feminist 'refusenik' who 'refuses to join an army of automatons in the name of Allah', and states in a public address to Muslims:

> In this letter, I am asking questions from which we can no longer hide. Why are we being held hostage by what's happening between the Palestinians and the Israelis? What's with the stubborn streak of anti-Semitism in Islam? Who is the real colonizer of

> Muslims—America or Arabia? Why are we squandering the talents of women, fully half of God's creation? (Manji 2003)

These questions function within a larger political climate in which Muslims are being incarcerated, bombed, and brutalised by the most militarised States in the world. Another example comes from Mona Eltahawy, who argues that the 'real' war in the Middle East is against the women: 'What hope can there be for women in the Egyptian parliament, dominated as it is by men stuck in the seventh century?... The hatred of women goes deep in Egyptian society' (Eltahawy 2012). As 'immigrants' in the West, people of colour, including Muslims, are treated as perpetual outsiders, but as anti-Islam activists amidst the war on terror, their work has been promoted, funded, and widely disseminated by State institutions, media, and women's and gender studies departments.

The desire that runs through the phantasmic construct of 'Islam', from which these feminists seek to 'rescue' the equally phantasmic Muslim woman, appeared in a most dramatic fashion in this genre of feminist politics: 'As a feminist, I have long dreamed of rescuing women who are trapped in domestic and sexual slavery against their will with no chance of escape', Chesler wrote, explaining her desire in an early defense of the US-led invasion of Afghanistan (2003: 198).[5] Here is the view of Sally Armstrong, another seasoned feminist, Canadian journalist and human rights advocate, well known for her decades of feminist activism in Afghanistan:

> They [Afghan women] have been playing on the back of my eyelids like old movies, the images of these women and girls I met during the last 11 years in Afghanistan. It has at times felt as much like a crusade as a journalistic assignment. (Armstrong, quoted in Shanahan 2009)

This self-projection as a 'feminist crusader' and Armstrong's implicit identification with the Christian wars against Islam has gone uncontested within feminist networks associated with international human rights work.

Such a framing of Islam and Muslim women is, of course, not new in the history of the West, or indeed in the feminist movements of the past. However, these histories were contested and deconstructed by decades of anti-racist and anti-colonial feminist movements and scholarship. Shunting aside these critiques, the reiteration of Orientalist tropes within contemporary feminist circuits endowed greater legitimacy to the demonisation of Islam in the global war on terror, even as such activism extended the reach of feminists and their organisations across national and international spheres of influence. The access Western feminists had acquired to the institutions of the State and media during the 1990s now allowed them to effectively marginalise anti-racist and anti-colonial discourses. The feminist subject was redefined as a future-oriented, intrinsically Western subject, the embodiment of its highest cultural values, gender egalitarianism. Critics have addressed the activities of particular feminist and human rights organisations involved in mobilising support for the war on terror, including, for example, the US Feminist Majority Foundation and the network Women for Afghan Women.[6] The point that is often overlooked, however, is how such feminist activism renewed the alliance between feminists and the (imperialist) State, a relation that extended the dissemination of these (pro-imperialist) feminist ideas and influence within the nation space and in global politics. The subject position of 'the feminist'—shorn of anti-racist or anti-colonial investments—was now readily available to Western populations, men as well as women, to claim as their own.[7]

The Innocence of War

The second feminist response identified in my early research centred on the concept of 'precarity', that is, the idea that the post-9/11 (Western) subject had been propelled into a heightened state of vulnerability, and that this is 'the human condition'. This iteration of feminist politics was advanced by Judith Butler, a foundational feminist thinker in the post-structural/modern theoretical tradition. Butler's development of the idea of 'precarity' in her theorisation of this war has had a transformative impact on feminist thinkers, including feminists of colour.

Opposing the US State's suspension of law in its invasion of Iraq, Butler argued in *Precarious Life* (2004) that the attacks of 9/11 demanded an ethical and moral response—not war—to the 'voice' of the 'Other'. In this context, Butler asks: How to build community in this condition of violence? More specifically, how to counter the divisive politics of the Iraq War? The 9/11 attacks, she explained, revealed 'the conditions of heightened vulnerability and aggression' (Butler 2004: xi), conditions that were further exacerbated by the Iraq War as well as the related erosion of civil rights within the US. This condition of 'heightened vulnerability', Butler went on to explain, was central to the human condition—from infancy, human beings are dependent on care from others and hence highly vulnerable to violence. The war had only intensified this vulnerability by demonstrating the 'precarity' of life itself.

Unlike other feminist interventions in the global war, Butler's approach to the invasion of Iraq was informed by Western philosophical, political, and psychoanalytic traditions. Her analysis, however, took as its starting point the injury done to the Self (the US nation-State) by its Other (defined as Muslim). Thus, her framing of the Iraq War—as *retaliatory* violence by the American State for the 9/11 attacks—presented the Muslim Other as the violent aggressor. It should be remembered that no direct link was established between the Iraqi regime led by Saddam Hussein, and al-Qaeda, which had claimed responsibility for the attack.

As I have discussed elsewhere (Thobani 2007), Butler's centring of the experience of the US subject in her reflections on Iraq deflected attention from the US-led Afghan War, as well as violence perpetrated by the US State in the decades preceding 9/11, including, most directly, the First Gulf War (1990–1991) and the drastic sanctions imposed on Iraq in its aftermath. Moreover, the concept of 'precarity' privileged the Western subject as the political prototype of the 'human'; Butler's discussion of an abstract 'infanthood' ascribed innocence to this Subject. This innocence was the grounds for its 'vulnerability'. Butler thus dehistoricised the conditions of 'being', so to speak, and used this as a frame for analysing the Iraq War. Precariousness is treated as a shared human experience, equally distributed.[8] My critique of this concept, centered on Butler's universalisation of West-centric vulnerability as 'the human condition', noted how this accomplishes—whether wittingly or not is not my concern—a dehistoricisation, de-racialisation, and de-gendering of this Subject as well as its Other (Thobani 2007). Such universalisation casts the Western subject as external to the US nation-State and its imperialist formation to instead situate it primarily within the (Eurocentric) psychoanalytic field, which privileges the condition of 'infancy', likewise universalised from a particular Western experience.

Butler's analysis of imperialist war, colonial occupation, and the catastrophic destruction of national sovereignty in Iraq reframed these events as a concern arising from a 'shared' primal, pre-individuated condition. Positing a commonality based on the Western subject's experience of the 'human' condition transforms the 'Other' into the Self-same and simultaneously distances them as the 'aggressive' Other. Butler's theorisation erases the historical experience of subjugation and resistance of this Other, Muslim in this case, and further, erases its political demands. The Western Self is here reinstated into the position of centrality, that is, into the epistemically violent position of determining what constitutes *the* universal condition for the human, while ejecting from the analytic-theoretical field the anti-imperialist and anti-colonial politics of the Other. Acceptance of the 'human condition' of the Western subject's 'precarity' becomes the condition of possibility for the building of community.

The concept of 'precarious' life, along with its various iterations as 'disposable', 'dispensible', 'vulnerable' life now proliferates in the field of women's and gender studies. This concept restores the (primal) state of innocence of the Western female subject while making illegible the vulnerability of Muslim women and men: to the wars of the US and its allied States; to catastrophic violence and sudden displacement; to border control and surveillance technologies; and, in the case of diasporic Muslims in the West, to the racial and religious profiling implemented by the security apparatus of these States.

Reinstating Global Sisterhood

The third approach in the feminist engagement with the global war is defined by the concept of 'gender apartheid', which became very popular in feminist discussion of the oppression of Afghan/Muslim women. The ideas associated with this concept were most substantively developed in the work of the feminists who sought to ally themselves with Afghan women on the basis of 'global sisterhood'. The concept is most cogently articulated in Zillah Eisenstein's book, *Against Empire* (2004). Here, Eisenstein identified the US as an imperial State, presented her anti-imperialist critique, and delineated the grounds for feminist solidarity. This was a promising start, but Eisenstein argued that the war on terror was grounded in patriarchal violence which took the form of 'sexual terrorism' in the US and 'gender apartheid' in Afghanistan. Recounting the racism and class exploitation that have shaped the history of US capitalism, Eisenstein then turned to the violence of the Taliban regime against Afghan women, such as its decision to ban women from public spaces, which she defined as 'gender apartheid'. Dismissing the idea of a cultural 'clash' between 'East and West', Eisenstein identified both the US and Afghan States as patriarchal entities perpetuating masculine violence. This 'patriarchy-in-common' created the conditions for alliance between US and Afghan women, on the basis of their supposedly shared experience of this violence.

The idea of a shared feminist politics between US and Afghan women elevated gender to a position of primacy, reconceptualising imperialist war as a 'clash of masculinities', as it were, dispensed with Eisenstein's earlier discussion of US racism and imperialism. Moreover, the idea that the status and experience of White women in the US is essentially the same as that of Afghan/Muslim women in a 'global patriarchy' or 'global misogyny' makes invisible colonial histories, the North/South divide, as well as the US-led domination of the Middle East and Central Asia; this idea also obscures the unequal power relations between Western and Afghan women, and more significantly, the role of Western women in the exploitation of the nation-States in the Global South. In short, such a feminist politics obfuscates the power hierarchy between unequally situated communities of women in the contemporary global order. Also significant here is the appropriation of the term 'apartheid', which specifically refers to a form of racial violence against both women *and* men in South Africa.

Eisenstein's subsequent work, *Sexual Decoys* (2007), continues the feminist elevation of gender above the other axes of power that organise the international order. As she explains in the earlier work,

> masculinist militarism uses women's rights for right wing agendas inside and outside the West. Right-wing fundamentalisms of all sorts—east and west—emphasize militarist agendas alongside the gendering of women's lives, with or without the veil/chador/abayya/burqa, as decoy. (Eisenstein 2004: 2)

The idea that 'Woman' is the real target of imperialism, militarism, terrorism, and 'right-wing' fundamentalisms, which are all subsumed under the rubric 'masculinist militarism', is further consolidated in this work.

The three trends I have identified as shaping feminist engagements with the war on terror have only deepened over time. Although these feminists draw on different theoretical traditions, and the political praxis associated with these traditions varies considerably, they are all marked by a collective sidelining of the anti-racist and anti-imperialist *feminist* critiques developed by women of colour. There is no shortage of such counter-hegemonic work, and its neglect is no insignificant matter.

It is a rare occasion indeed when Western feminists engage with critiques of the West that are produced by non-Western scholars, especially women of colour. This is particularly true for critiques of Western politics grounded in the historical experiences of Muslims. I now turn to just such an engagement to illustrate how critiques of the West are negotiated—and neutralised—to re-establish the feminist orthodoxies, hegemonies, and hierarchies that privilege Western tradition. Such critiques are engaged with only when the challenge to Western power becomes urgent, I argue, which in this case, was a result of the political upheavals wrought by the global war and the resistance to it.

Constraining the Other

The construction of the West as a defender of rights and freedoms against an 'irrationally intolerant' Islam and 'hate-filled', 'fanatical' Muslims became particularly charged upon the publication of a Danish cartoon that represented the Prophet of Islam as a terrorist in 2005.[9] As Muslims around the world expressed outrage and organised demonstrations against this depiction, Western elites (politicians, intellectuals, media, as well as feminists) argued that the principle at stake here was the right to free speech of the Danish magazine and its readership, which they associated with the future of democracy in Europe. Muslims were therefore publicly denounced as intolerant bigots and medieval fanatics for deeming the cartoon 'blasphemous'. How the West could even 'tolerate' the presence of these Muslims became a burning question in the political furore that followed. This is the context for the exchange that I discuss below. I can only present here a partial reading of this exchange, and will therefore focus on the part that dealt specifically with the idea of free speech (for a detailed account of the full exchange, see Thobani 2017).

The exchange was centred on the question: 'Is Critique Secular?' The implicit assumption (given the political climate) was that Muslims are neither critics nor secular. Talal Asad, one of the interlocutors, questioned the binary on which the debate was based: tolerant West versus intolerant Islam (Asad et al. 2009). Challenging the idea of the 'self-owning individual' and 'free speech', he noted these are not absolute, and in any case had emerged historically as bourgeois demands tied to the rise of capitalism. Asad instead identified racism as a major factor driving the European public's responses to Muslims who opposed publication of the cartoon. In the global context, colonialism and imperialism were crucial to the development of Euro-American secularism, which shaped the relation of the West to the 'Rest'. In light of these histories, as Asad argues, '[i]t is not easy, therefore, to understand exactly what is being claimed when "democracy" and "free speech" are said to be intrinsic to "European civilization", and inequality and repression are attributed to "Islamic civilization"....' (ibid.: 24). Saba Mahmood (ibid.), who also participated in the discussion, pointed to the Protestant underpinnings of the Western understanding of blasphemy, and also argued that the racialisation of Muslims as minorities put them at a structural disadvantage in European societies, where the State protected and elevated the interests of majorities.

Judith Butler responded to both these analyses. The resulting discussions are layered and cover much ground but it is her response to Asad's critique of 'free speech' that is of interest here. Butler's intervention defended the right to 'free speech', and where Asad opened up space to rethink the binary formulations (civilised West/uncivilised Islam; freedom/tyranny; rights/repression) in public discourse, Butler closed this down by reinvigorating the binary between the Western subject as 'freedom'-oriented and the Muslim as orientated towards oppression. She did this by calling on 'progressives' to support freedom of speech, which she argued is vital to the protection of the rights of sexual/gender minorities (Asad et al. 2009: 127). In this manner, Butler elided the arguments presented by Asad and Mahmood for rethinking the binary formulation of the West and the Rest, the histories of their making, as well as their critique of how 'critical thought'—as defined within this Western tradition—was itself part of this history. Instead, Butler's response sutures over the ruptures in the narrative of Western exceptionalism that Asad's critique accomplished by highlighting 'free speech' as key among liberal governing practices.

The issue of free speech has divided the left, Butler notes, leaving LGBTQIAP+ communities in a quandary. Free speech and opposition to censorship 'have clearly been cornerstones of the movement for decades,' she argues, so

> it is quite understandable that there might be a strong group of sexual progressives who maintain that freedom of expression is essential to the movement, that the lesbian, gay, bi, trans, queer, intersex movement is not possible without freedom of expression and without recourse to freedom itself as a guiding value and norm. (Asad et al. 2009: 127)

Butler's explication of queer identity politics sets it up as oppositional to, not in affiliation with, the rights of Muslims who were under attack across Euro-America through this very issue of 'free' speech. Implicit in her presentation of gender/sexual politics was the assumption that queer Muslims either do not exist, or if they do, warrant no particular attention, and that queer political movements are monolithic and Western.

The principle of free speech '...does not answer the questions of whether and how that norm is to be reconciled with other norms, nor does it tell us precisely what is meant by "freedom,"' Butler acknowledges (Asad et al. 2009: 127). Yet, she maintained her point that it is imperative that this freedom be defended, even if its meaning remains 'unclear'. Presumably this should be the case even if such a defense intensifies public antagonisms towards Muslim communities under siege by the violence of the liberal-democratic state. The Eurocentric, racial, and liberal *political* leanings of this feminist/queer philosophical position are evident in such an argument. The discursive move here is the insertion of gender/sexuality as presenting *legitimate* concerns regarding the precarity of the queer subject, in contrast to the religio-racial (supposedly queer-free) struggles of Muslims against State-sanctioned violence. In this iteration of feminist/queer politics, the principle of free speech displaces the figure of the Muslim (presented as heteronormative and homophobic), and the figure of the queer person (assumed to be Western and White) emerges as emblematic of the 'vulnerable'—yet heroic—Subject of the moment.

Situating the White queer subject at the forefront of the Western politico-philosophical framework in Butler's response thus advances this tradition in a moment of global crisis. This occurs through a double move. *First*, it overrides the *critique* of liberal-capitalist freedoms presented in Asad's analysis of the historical and contemporary experience of Muslims, which reveals the violence of this liberal-secular order. *Second*, it collapses this counter-hegemonic critique into a *threat* to the 'freedom' of the Western queer subject. The White feminist/queer subject hence emerges as embodiment of the highest values of a now reworked Western tradition. Such neutralisation of critiques of the Western tradition relies on reification and refortification of its foundational concepts as *singularly* legitimate *and* of representing Muslims as requiring disciplining into the power of this tradition.

Conclusion

The representational strategies in the feminist/queer practices I have discussed in this chapter are foundational to the field of women's and gender studies, and they remain consistent across the range of texts I have analysed. I began this chapter by arguing that feminist thought and politics were in a state of crisis in the West, having lost considerable ground to the anti-racist and anti-colonial politics of women of colour by the closing decade of the twentieth century. This lost ground, I have argued, has been reclaimed by the post-9/11 gendering of Islamophobic discourses and racial constructs of Muslims, practices shared not only by neo-conservative and neoliberal political factions in the imperialist State, but also amongst feminist scholars and activists who draw from a range of theoretical traditions, including those of left and queer movements. The concepts of 'new anti-Semitism', 'gender apartheid', and 'precarity' now abound within the field of women's and gender studies, as does the linking of feminist and queer identities to the Westernising concepts of 'freedom' and 'free choice', presented in a binary with the misogyny and homophobia attributed to Islam and Muslims.

What these feminist engagements (and refusals to engage) accomplish for the underlying gender/sexual politics that shape the West can be summarised as follows. *First*, one finds the reiteration of longstanding gendered/racial colonial discourses and tropes, associated here singularly with Muslims and Islam. In the process, the idea of the cultural superiority of the West is recuperated, with gender constructed as the grounds of Western (that is, White) exceptionalism. Feminist representations of Muslims as 'anti-women' have become common sense, and as such, obscure the privileged location of White women in the global order; the power of hegemonic feminism is obfuscated and anti-colonial and anti-racist contestations of Western power are rendered unintelligible on gendered grounds. This *feminist power to represent* simultaneously recuperated the hegemonic position of Western feminism within the field of women's and gender studies and in the field of international feminist praxis.

Second, these feminist interventions led to a renewed alliance of feminism with the Western nation-State as based in shared values and identities, as can be seen most clearly in the identification of Muslims with the 'new' anti-Semitism or with the feminist delineation of the heightened 'precarity' of the Western subject. The feminist argument about 'gender apartheid' is slightly more nuanced as it recognises the violence directed at women in the West. Yet, this argument masks the Western State's racial/imperialist violence by representing it as directed only at 'Woman'. The deeper alliance between feminism and the Western nation-State relies on the former upholding the narrative of Western exceptionalism, directly undermining the transformative potential of anti-racist and anti-colonial politics of women/feminists of colour.

And *third*, the reiteration of feminist politics in the Orientalist vernaculars of the West (fanatic Muslims, the veil as imprisonment, gender apartheid, Western superiority, etc.) privileges gender as the base from which Western feminists can situate themselves at the forefront of a project to reconstitute the idea of the West *through* the global war against Muslims.

In contrast, anti-racist and anti-colonial politics are crucial to the success of trans/national solidarities and alliances that seek to undo the violence of the West. This entails a dismantling of its underlying racial/imperial power structure; none of the feminist texts I have discussed here envisage such a possibility. Instead, they project any gender egalitarian future as Western in its essence, and the future of the West as essentially pro-feminist. It remains to be seen how effective and sustainable these feminist practices, which re-stabilise Whiteness and posit a future of Westernity, shall be. But the global war has enabled Western feminism to reassert its dominance over the anti-racist and anti-colonial politics of women of colour, including Muslims. The role of women's and gender studies as a key battleground for these relations of power has only intensified as the war on terror morphs and advances into more regions at the international level.

Notes

1. President Bush's remarks at his administration's introduction of the Afghan Women and Children Act, 2001, directly linked the status of Afghan women to the US-led invasion of Afghanistan. See The White House (2001).

2. My earlier readings of a number of the feminist texts included in this chapter were published in Thobani (2007, 2010).

3. See also Hirschkind and Mahmood (2002).

4. See, for instance, François (2021) and Feder (2020).

5. In keeping with this imperial feminist fantasy, Chesler (2003) reveals that her own feminism was spurred by the hyper-patriarchy of the Muslim world, which she witnessed during the time she spent in Afghanistan.

6. See *Feminist Daily News* (2002). For example, speaking on behalf of 'more than 220 leading human rights and women's organizations in the U.S. and around the world' (ibid.), the Washington-based Feminist Majority Foundation not only backed the US invasion of Afghanistan, but also called on the Bush Administration to increase the number of American troops in Kabul and to extend their occupation across that country.

7. See Stolba (2002). The National Organization of Women, for another example, used the global war as an opportunity to strengthen the alliances between feminist and gay activism in the US. The organisation

> use[d] the terrorist attacks to flak its own domestic agenda, declaring that 'in this time of national and global turmoil, the reasons we celebrate "Coming Out Day" are more visible and important than ever' and proceeded to call for a permanent lifting of the ban on gays in the military. (Stolba 2002)

8. This is how Butler explains it: 'To be injured means that one has the chance to reflect upon injury, to find out the mechanisms of its distribution, to find out who else suffers from permeable borders, unexpected violence, dispossession, and fear, and in what ways'. (2004: xii)

9. For an interesting review of a range of political perspectives on the Danish cartoon controversy, see Laborde et al. (2011).

References

Amos, Valerie and Pratibha Parmar. 1984. 'Challenging Imperial Feminism'. *Feminist Review* 17 (1): 3–19.

Arat-Koc, S. 2002. 'Hot Potato: Imperial Wars or Benevolent Interventions? Reflections on Global Feminism Post September 11'. *Atlantis* 26 (2): 433–444.

Armstrong, Sally. 2003. *Daughters of Afghanistan*. Documentary film, written by Armstrong, directed by Robin Berger.

Asad, Talal, Wendy Brown, Judith Butler, and Saba Mahmood. 2009. *Is Critique Secular? Blasphemy, Injury, and Free Speech*. Berkeley: University of California Press.

Bannerji, H. 1995. *Thinking Through: Essays on Feminism, Marxism and Anti-Racism*. Toronto: Women's Press.

Barlas, A. 2002. *Believing Women in Islam*. Austin: University of Texas.

Butler, Judith. 2004. *Precarious Life: The Powers of Mourning and Violence*. London: Verso.

CBC News. 2019. 'Hijab-wearing Teacher Threatens to Leave Quebec if Secularism Bill Becomes Law'. *Canadian Broadcasting Corporation*, 28 March. Available at https://www.cbc.ca/news/canada/montreal/teacher-vows-to-leave-quebec-rather-than-take-off-her-headscarf-for-the-caq-1.5075942 (accessed January 2024).

Chesler, Phyllis. 2003. *The New Anti-Semitism: The Current Crisis and What We Must Do About It*. San Francisco: Jossey-Bass.

______. 2010. 'Ban the Burqa? Argument in Favour'. *Middle East Quarterly* 17 (4): 33–45.

Crenshaw, Kimberley. 1991. 'Mapping the Margins: Intersectionality, Identity Politics and Violence against Women of Colour'. *Stanford Law Review* 43 (6): 1241–1299.

Davis, Angela. 1983. *Women, Race and Class*. New York: Random House.

Eisenstien, Zillah. 2004. *Against Empire: Feminisms, Racisms and the West*. London: Zed Books.

______. 2007. *Sexual Decoys: Gender, Race and War in Imperial Democracy*. London: Zed Books.

Eltahawy, Mona. 2012. 'Why Do They Hate Us? The Real War on Women is in the Middle East'. *Foreign Policy*. Available at https://foreignpolicy.com/2012/04/23/why-do-they-hate-us/ (accessed April 2024).

Feder, Sandra. 2020. 'Stanford Scholars Report French Headscarf Ban Adversely Affects Muslim Girls'. *Stanford School of Humanities and Social Sciences*, 25 August. Available at https://humsci.stanford.edu/feature/stanford-scholars-report-french-headscarf-ban-adversely-impacts-muslim-girls (accessed January 2024).

Feminist Daily News. 2002. 'Eleanor Smeal Urges President to Fulfil Promise to Afghan Women'. *Feminist Majority Foundation*. Available at https://feminist.org/news/press/eleanor-smeal-urges-president-to-fulfill-promise-to-afghan-women/ (accessed November 2023).

François, Myriam. 2021. '"I Felt Violated by the Demand to Undress": Three Muslim Women on France's Hostility to the Hijab'. *The Guardian*, 27 July. Available at https://www.theguardian.com/world/2021/jul/27/i-felt-violated-by-the-demand-to-undress-three-muslim-women-on-frances-hostility-to-the-hijab (accessed January 2024).

Harris, Cheryl. 1993. 'Whiteness as Property'. *Harvard Law Review* 106 (8): 1709–1791.

Hill Collins, Patricia. 1990. *Black Feminist Thought*. New York: Routledge.

Hirschkind, C., and S. Mahmood. 2002. 'Feminism, the Taliban, and Politics of Counter-Insurgency.' *Anthropological Quarterly* 75 (2): 339–354.

Hirsi-Ali, A. 2006. *The Caged Virgin: An Emancipation Proclamation for Women and Islam*. New York: The Free Press.

Laborde, Cecile, et al. 2011. 'Review: The Danish Cartoon Controversy and the Challenges of Multicultural Politics: A Discussion of the Cartoons that Shook the World'. *Perspectives on Politics* 9 (3): 603–619.

LaDuke, Winona. 1997. *Last Standing Woman*. Voyageur Press.

Lowe, Lisa. 1996. *Immigrant Acts: On Asian American Cultural Politics*. Durham: Duke University Press.

Manji, Irshad. 2003. *The Trouble with Islam Today*. Toronto: Random House.

Maracle, Lee. 1988. *I Am Woman: A Native Perspective on Sociology and Feminism*. Vancouver: Press Gang Publishers.

Monture Angus, P. 1995. *Thunder in My Soul*. Halifax: Fernwood Press.

Nicolas, Emilie. 2022. 'Insidious Impact of Bill 21 Goes Beyond Teachers Losing Jobs'. *The Gazette*, 21 March. Available at https://montrealgazette.com/opinion/columnists/nicolas-insidious-impact-of-bill-21-goes-beyond-teachers-losing-jobs (accessed January 2024).

Perry, Louise. 2019. 'How a Feminist Prophet became an Apostate: An Interview with Dr. Phyllis Chesler'. *Quillette*, 20 June. Available at https://quillette.com/2019/06/20/how-a-feminist-prophet-became-an-apostate-an-interview-with-dr-phyllis-chesler/ (accessed November 2023).

Pitts, Claudia. 2017. 'Phyllis Chesler: A Life on Behalf of Women'. *Women and Therapy* 40 (3–4): 288–300.

Razack, S., M. Smith, and S. Thobani (eds). 2010. *States of Race: Critical Race Feminism for the 21st Century*. Toronto: Between the Lines.

Scott, Joan Wallach. 2007. *Politics of the Veil*. New Jersey: Princeton University Press.

Shanahan, Noreen. 2009. 'Armstrong Continues Chronicles of Afghanistan Women'. *Herizons* (Fall issue): 45.

Smith, Malinda. 2010. 'Gender, Whiteness, and "other Others" in the Academy'. In *States of Race: Critical Race Feminism for the 21st Century*, S. Razack, M. Smith, and S. Thobani (eds): 37–58. Toronto: Between the Lines.

Stack, Liam. 2017. 'Burqa Bans: Which Countries Outlaw Face Coverings?' *The New York Times*, 19 October. Available at https://www.nytimes.com/217/10/19/world/europe/quebec-burqa-ban-europe.html (accessed November 2023).

Stolba, Carol. 2002. 'Feminists Go to War', *The Women's Quarterly* (Winter), *Independent Women's Forum*. Available at https://web.archive.org/web/20030831034002/http://www.iwf.org/pubs/twq/Winter2002i.shtml (accessed January 2024).

Thobani, Sunera. 2002. 'War Frenzy'. *Meridiens: Feminism, Race, Transnationalism* 2 (2): 289–297.

______. 2007. 'White Wars: Western Feminism and the "War on Terror"'. *Feminist Theory*: 169–185.

______. 2010. 'White Innocence, Western Supremacy: The Role of Western Feminism in the "War on Terror"'. In *States of Race: Critical Race Feminism for the 21st Century*, S. Razack, M. Smith, and S. Thobani (eds): 127–146. Toronto: Between the Lines.

______. 2017. 'The Secularity of Empire, the Violence of Critique'. *Hypatia* 32 (3): 715–730.

______. 2022. *Coloniality and Racial (In)Justice in the University: Counting for Nothing?* Toronto: University of Toronto Press.

Torres, Lourdes, Chandra Mohanty, and Ann Russo (eds). 1991. *Third World Women and the Politics of Feminism*. Bloomington: Indiana University Press.

White House, The. 2001. 'President Signs Afghan Women and Children Relief Act'. December. Available at https://georgewbush-whitehouse.archives.gov/news/releases/2001/12/20011212-9.html (accessed January 2024).

7

Women's Studies is Dead! Long Live Women's Studies!

Panchali Ray

By now, it has been largely accepted that feminism shares a fraught relationship with institutions. Of course, I am not suggesting that feminism should be a set of free-floating ideas that is completely independent of social, economic, and political institutions; instead I argue that feminism is produced, as well as constrained, by institutions. When thinking about feminism and institutions, it is imperative to reflect on the institutional politics of knowledge production. For instance, this is not just a question of excluding women, but also a question of what have been or continue to be the implications when women are included. While the ongoing struggle to include women in institutions continues, the efficacy of a full-fledged degree-granting programme such as women's studies remains under question. Unlike other disciplines, a women's studies programme has more clarity on the subject of its study. This is reflected not just in its name, but also the history of its institutionalisation, its relationship with the women's movements, and the vision of its founders, which together make obvious that a women's studies programme has the goal of not just making women visible in knowledge production but also initiating action that would question phallogocentrism.

At its inception, women's studies was seen not as a discipline but a perspective that would re-orient knowledge production and reflect women's experiences and voices within patriarchal academic structures. The growth of women's studies into a discipline has been well documented, including its phenomenal expansion and the challenges it continues to face institutionally (see the Introduction to this volume). This chapter will explore the challenges that newer forms of theorisation and activism, particularly post-structuralist interventions to the category 'woman', have posed to 'traditional' Women's Studies Centres (WSCs). The tension between the abstract 'woman' and the empirical category informs much of the contestations over designing of syllabi and the possibilities of institutionalisation. In India, while theoretical debates have come to accept the overdetermination of the category 'woman', which makes it impossible to speak of a universal, homogenous category, the commitment of a women's studies programme to its historical legacy and roots necessitates retaining the category.

Education and the Neoliberal Academy

The Indian educational apparatus and its ideological and political growth is deeply rooted in the country's colonial past, whether it is T. B. Macaulay's Minute of 1835 and William Bentinck's support of its recommendations, or even earlier proposals such as the one by Charles Grant in 1797 that was dismissive of 'indigenous' knowledge and cultural practices (Stokes 1959). While the East India Company initially restrained itself from interfering too much with education systems, by the early nineteenth century, with its supremacy well established, it confidently introduced educational reforms, amongst others. Whether as an initiative of the colonial administration or commercial policies of the Company and its successful twining with evangelism, education became an important method of assimilation (ibid.).

Subsequently, despite an avowed commitment to vernacular language and regional knowledge production in policy, such ideas were dismissed in practice. The universities that opened in the Presidencies (Madras, Calcutta, and Bombay) gave primacy to the English language and emerging professional opportunities meant that there were more and more takers for English language education, the effects of which still resonate in contemporary India.

In fact, access to English language education has been one of the key axes for the reinforcement of power accruing from class and caste location. Further, scholars have defined the middle class as a group of people who have risen in power and prestige due to their access to scarce resources such as education and occupational skills (Bardhan 1994; Deshpande 2004). It is understood that the emergence of the middle class is bound up with the development of capitalism, where as a social group they provided various services for the maintenance of the system. In Bengal, for instance, the emergence of the middle class was tied to land ownership, as colonial rule disintegrated native industries (Mukhopadhyay 1998; Tripathi 1994). The introduction of English education to help the British run the colonial administrative machinery with ease meant that it was this class, by sheer dint of possessing cultural capital, who took to modern English education. Thus, English education became a key ingredient in the formation of the Bengali middle class. As scholars have argued, the Indian Universities Act of 1905 further consolidated the dominance of the British government in the field of higher education, angering nationalists who in turn founded educational institutions of their own, subsequently generating debates on what constituted a 'national' education (Ghosh 2000). The distancing from land and manual labour and inclination towards *chakri* (jobs), preferably government services, marked the disposition of this new class (Mukhopadhyay 1998). Even in contemporary times, entry to the ranks of middle class is contingent on taste, refinement, education, and the ability to hoard cultural capital whether through institutional means, social networking, or gatekeeping (Bourdieu 1984).

The development of educational institutions from colonial to contemporary India is produced by this context, whether in terms of churning out individuals for the job market or reinforcing the superiority of the English language as the preferred mode of communication. With independence, the Indian State promoted higher education as an instrument for achieving social equality, and there was a phenomenal expansion of higher educational institutions. However, with time, there was a decrease in government spending and the State's gradual withdrawal from the sector has led to privatisation, which fuelled an increase in management, engineering, and technical courses and a corresponding decline in social sciences and humanities (Patel 2004). Sujata Patel further points out that the establishment of new trade regimes (General Agreement on Trade in Services and World Trade Organization) and the entry of foreign universities or their franchisee have deeply affected the quality of education offered, which runs contrary to the idea of 'national' education as envisaged by the country's founding fathers (ibid.). Other scholars have also observed the adverse effect of globalisation on education. For instance, Morrow and Torres (2000) argue that historically, the State had autonomy in shaping public education, but this is now being eroded with increasing interference by institutions such as World Bank and United Nations Educational, Scientific and Cultural Organization (UNESCO).

With privatisation, the concept of education has undergone a change: Critical thinking has been replaced by the necessity of literacy and education as a mode to increase capacity and productivity of human beings. This has become a predominant trend in the developmental paradigm (Kumar 2006). Simultaneously, social attitudes and the developmentalist agenda of the country meant that resources were often directed towards technical colleges and universities, like the Indian Institutes of Technology, and not humanities and social sciences (Padmanabhan and Tilak 1986). With allocation of funds to higher education decreasing, universities and other institutions of higher education are under mounting pressure to mobilise resources through other means, such as floating self-financing courses (Indira 2006). Thus, education emerges not as a social good but a profitable venture. It has been argued that the education system has lost its capability to produce 'organic intellectuals', and instead focuses on producing workers for the job market (Patnaik 2005). K. N. Panikkar (2002) argues that the privatisation of education meant that the education system would be oriented to meet the demands of the advanced capitalist countries, and that the Indian education system would produce workers for transnational capital. Thus, education is no longer a tool for social equality but a commodity to be purchased

(Pathy 2003). It is in this larger context and historical trajectory that one must place the emergence, expansion, and consolidation of WSCs.

The Emergence of Women's Studies in India

Women's studies emerged in the mid-1980s in India, propelled by a multitude of academic and activist initiatives that sought to centre the category 'woman' in order to understand and challenge patriarchy in both cultural spheres and the political economy. Thus, from its birth, women's studies had a clear goal of social transformation. A seminal report by the Committee on the Status of Women in India titled *Towards Equality* (1974) brought to the fore the dismal situation of women in the country despite three decades of independence. This rude awakening, coupled with other factors, including academic initiatives by the Indian Council of Social Science Research (ICSSR) (1975) propelled the emergence of women's studies programmes. In 1979, when the ICSSR Committee on women's studies reviewed the programmes it had initiated, they felt that while there was some impact on policy and advocacy, as a whole 'it had failed to make any substantial impact on the community of social scientists and the major institutions undertaking social science research' (Mazumdar 2010: 8). Apart from these academic initiatives, the autonomous women's movement in the early 1970s and 1980s demanded separate academic spaces to research and teach feminist theories that would rejuvenate the women's movements and vice versa, and thus, the Indian Association for Women's Studies (IAWS) was formed in 1982. However, one must note that prior to all these developments, in 1974, the Shreemati Nathibai Damodar Thackersey (SNDT) Women's University opened a Women's Studies Centre. Therefore, even before the findings of the *Towards Equality* report or institutional initiatives were widely reported, there was already a 'fundamental shift', in Mary John's words, 'from women as subjects to be educated to "women" as new subjects of investigation and study' (John 2008: 4). Responding to these various demands, the University Grants Commission (UGC) too started taking initiatives to streamline WSCs in the university structure, and beginning from 1986, centres and cells in colleges/universities were established with the support of subsequent Five Year Plans (for a detailed recording and documentation of the emergence of the discipline, see Jain and Rajput 2003; John 2002; Krishna Raj 1986; and Pappu 2002).

Women's studies, in its earlier conceptualisation, was perceived 'as an instrument for women's development and also as a necessary input to deepen the knowledge base of various disciplines.... women's studies has to be understood not merely in the context of research and teaching but also action' (Krishna Raj 1986: 20). Thus, women's studies was to be instrumental for both knowledge production as well as challenging patriarchal structures. Over the years, these centres played a critical role in shaping policies in social and economic arenas that included labour, livelihood, education, population control, political participation (reservations in local government bodies), violence against women, sexuality, rights, etc. With consistent campaigns, research, documentation, and teaching, WSCs were able to influence policy, law, and developmental agendas. Simultaneously, WSCs have sought to orient different disciplines toward the question of gender. In particular, the disciplines of literary studies, history, sociology, law, and development economics have responded to this by reconceptualising some of their basic tenets (Patel 2005). However, despite the transformative potential of the lens of gender for different disciplines, women's studies has suffered from a certain ghettoisation. Thus, it has often been reduced to a mere 'paper' or 'topic' on women in the syllabi of various college and university departments, even as the pedagogic focus within these disciplines remains untouched by any critical thinking about gender. And, as Mary John (2008) further argues, assessing the impact of women's studies on higher education is still difficult and elusive. Whatever be the impact of women's studies on different disciplines and departments, its future remains uncertain. The last few years have seen a gradual decline in funding allocated to WSCs. While the central government maintains an ambiguous stand in its vision for the future of interdisciplinary centres, state-funded universities have also not shown any interest in expanding women's studies into full departments, hiring full-time faculty, or releasing research grants.

Discipline or Outreach Programme? The Tension Between Women's 'Studies' and 'Movements'

A genuinely liberatory women's studies classroom is one that aims to question all forms of oppression, whether based on patriarchy, race, caste, class, or sexuality. Given the emphasis on education as a commodity that produces 'skilled' workers to fit into the knowledge-driven global economy, women's studies classrooms, with their ambivalence towards such modes of employment, provide a space for radical questioning and thinking. Often referred to as the 'intellectual arm of the women's movement', the feminist syllabi of WSCs is rooted in modernism with an interventionist approach aimed at the emancipation of women.

The institutionalisation of women's studies in the formal academy raises many questions: the early years witnessed discussions on whether women's studies is a discipline or a perspective. The establishment of UGC-supported centres and its phenomenal growth, particularly under the Twelfth Five Year Plan remains in conflict with the original mandate of women's studies as a perspective. In this context, one must reflect on both the politics of institutionalising radical theory—which questions the very norms by which one lives—and the political economy in which it flourishes. When one thinks of feminism, a set of fundamental questions is often raised. How does one theorise 'being' into knowledge? What does thinking mean? At what point does thinking become an 'ism', a profession, and an institution? Thinking as what? Can we think professionally and in a compartmentalised manner? The professionalisation of feminism requires 'truth' telling: a 'truth' that exists and which one must uncover. A commitment to the women's movement, to a pre-defined goal of emancipation implies that feminism becomes instrumental, practical, mechanical, and goal-oriented, and thus thinking becomes rooted in acting and doing.

The university has never been a hospitable space for WSCs, often eyeing them with suspicion as 'too' political and not academic 'enough'. Despite such antagonism, it has allowed their establishment; however, as scholars have noted, they remain in the margins across the world, often reliant on the under/un-paid labour of temporarily hired teachers and with research scholars teaching large parts of the syllabi (Skeggs 1995). It is my observation and personal experience that in India, despite the UGC's mandate, universities do not adhere to an equivalent pay scale for teaching and non-teaching staff hired contractually by WSCs. Recruited under the UGC plan period scheme, faculty and research scholars of WSCs often find themselves ghettoised, overworked, and financially exploited by even the most prestigious public universities in the country. In fact, over the years there has been a systematic decline in funding for WSCs. In 2019, when the National Democratic Alliance (NDA) government returned to power, the UGC issued new guidelines that drastically cut down the budget for all 200 WSCs by 40 per cent (Singh 2019). This instability makes WSCs vulnerable to budget cuts and possibilities of closure in uncertain times, particularly during change in political regimes. This also means that faculty members, too busy simply trying to survive, often focus on funded projects to keep the centres alive at the expense of initiating work that could push the boundaries of academic scholarship. For instance, while the establishment currently remains unsympathetic to women's studies, and with no surety of continuity of funds (*Deccan Chronicle* 2019), making teaching and research unsustainable, WSCs are often asked to conduct gender sensitisation courses for research scholars and faculty members. This fits into the mandate of a neoliberal regime that perceives education as a means of producing good 'subjects'. The role of women's studies, then, is to produce citizens who fit into the global economy, embodying gendered values that reflect the country's modernity and its break with its feudal past. It, however, remains at odds with critical thinking that could open up the possibilities of questioning norms that create and sustain phallogocentrism.

On the contrary, beyond the university, women's studies has often been seen as a discipline that has taken from the women's movements and not given back. A debt not paid. Feminist scholarship is now perceived to have become 'too theoretical' and not connected with the lives and struggles of the woman 'out there' in the 'real' world. bell hooks argues that without feminist theory, there can be no liberatory politics and feminism within the 'corporate' university space where both teachers and students come from middle-class, White, elite backgrounds, must shoulder the responsibility of challenging patriarchal university structures, as well as reach out to the masses of women who have no access to such privileged spaces. Thus, it is imperative that feminism challenge the boundaries of disciplines, particularly the ones that value White, Eurocentric knowledge production (hooks 1989).

While it is well-established that feminist epistemology has the potential to break down mainstream knowledge production, feminist theory, when disciplined within the structures of women's studies departments and centres, is unable to negotiate the tension that often accompanies institutionalisation of knowledge. For instance, the term 'academic feminism' is often used to berate feminists who are seen as detached from reality, confined to specific niches, and not concerned with the everyday lives of women. Since feminism is often seen as a political endeavour and not an academic one, the term 'academic feminism' denotes a 'betrayal'—a betrayal of feminist politics. There exists a double bind, where on the one hand feminism is not perceived as 'sufficiently' academic, given its commitment to pre-defined goals and agendas, and on the other, the charge of 'academic feminists' is levied on those who are perceived to be no longer concerned with *changing* women's lives. In fact, Kumud Sharma argues that mainstreaming women's studies has had the counter-effect of placing it within a web of complex relationships and hierarchies. Firmly embedded within the inflexible university structure, far from questioning patriarchal power, women's studies scholars and faculty often reproduce the hierarchies rampant within the universities (Sharma 2003).

The 'Woman' in Women's Studies

The establishment of women's studies emerged from a radical environment of critical scholarship that questioned the very foundations of knowledge production. However, one must inject a note of caution and ask: How is critique bound up with power? Judith Butler argues that

> the exercise of critique typically takes place through the formulation of a set of questions… can we think about how, under certain conditions, certain kinds of questions *cannot* be posed or, rather, can only be framed and posed by breaking through a certain prohibition that functions to condition and circumscribe the domain of the speakable. (Butler 2009: 776, emphasis in original)

Thus, today, one can safely argue that women's studies is equally imbued with radical and conservative impulses. Given the expansive domain of scholarship that has questioned the category 'woman', rarely do faculty and scholars of WSCs want to let go of the subject. According to Wendy Brown,

> women's studies as a contemporary institution, however, may be politically and theoretically incoherent, as well as tacitly conservative—incoherent because by definition it circumscribes, uncircumscribable 'women' as an object of study, and conservative because it must resist all objections to such circumscription if it is to sustain that object of study as its *raison d'etre*… theory that destabilises the category of women, racial formations that disrupt the unity or primacy of the category, and sexualities that similarly blur the solidarity of the category—each of these must be restricted, resisted, or worse, colonised to preserve the realm. (Brown 1997: 84)

This disciplining of women's studies, imperative for it to be recognised as a discipline within the academic structure, requires exclusions, borders, and boundedness of subjects of inquiry. The object of study must be fixed and adhered to with a fierce commitment. Brown further argues that fields of inquiry premised on social identities often find themselves in troubled waters when that identity is itself questioned:

> Thus, paradoxically, sustaining gender as a critical, self-reflexive category rather than a normative or nominal one, and sustaining women's studies as an intellectually and institutionally radical site rather than a regulatory one—in short refusing to allow gender and women's studies to be disciplined—are concerns and refusals at odd with affirming women's studies *as* a coherent field of study. (ibid.: 86, emphasis in original)

In an influential essay on the institutionalisation of women's studies, Jacques Derrida asks, 'Do the women who manage these programs, do they not become, in turn, the guardians of the law, and do they not risk constructing an institution similar to the institution against which they are fighting?' (Derrida 2003 [1987]: 190). Derrida proposes that the Law is a pre-condition—a logos that produces and sustains institutions—and that those who guard institutions must also be guardians of the Law. So while women's studies gains legitimacy within institutions, its proponents too must assume the roles of guardian and gatekeeper, and thus, in the last count adhere to phallogocentrism. Despite its best intentions, women's studies, according to Derrida, becomes nothing more than 'another cell in the university beehive' (ibid: 191).

Women's studies in India is known to have subscribed to a very narrow understanding of what the category 'woman' stands for. Not as an empty signifier, but one which works within the framework of the sex-gender system. This has often led to WSCs being accused of casteism, homophobia, and transphobia. The push to rename 'Women's Studies' as 'Gender and Sexuality Studies' comes partly from male feminists and the queer community, who argue that given the fluidity of gender, retaining the category 'woman' is exclusionary and regressive as the focus remains on the materiality of the biological woman, with no significant acknowledgment of the signification system that produces the 'male' and the 'female'. In this context, male feminists have often used standpoint theory to try and understand men's alliance with feminism. The concept of standpoint, according to Sandra Harding, 'is not a perspective; it does not just flow spontaneously from the condition of women's existence. It has to be wrested out against the hegemonic dominant ideologies that structure the practices of daily life' (Harding 1998: 185). This idea defies any easy correlation of biology with identity, ideology, and marginality. In fact, in Harding's view, standpoint implies a struggle against the doxic, the commonplace. As much as 'woman' is not a homogenous category, deeply divided by internal differences, the category 'man' is also divided in its differential access to power and privileges in a phallogocentric society.

Thus, one can safely argue that men's relation to feminism would possibly entail, at best, recognition and distancing from hetero-patriarchal privileges that govern the daily life of elite, cis-gender, heterosexual men. At worst, it can be seen as an alliance that differing and sometimes antagonistic social groups share, such as when upper-caste people rally in support of anti-caste struggles, or when men, without identifying themselves as feminists, work to bring in legal and social reform. In India, the historical trajectory of the social reform movement, particularly in the nineteenth century, is often identified with and led by male reformers—however contentious, this does bring into sharp focus the role of men and their relation to women's emancipation. The increase in enrolment of cis-gender men from marginalised caste, class, and queer communities[1] in women's studies classrooms implies a certain connection between social location and ideologies of resistance. While I am aware that some self-identified 'male feminists' who have institutionally gained power come from elite backgrounds and rarely question the histories of their privileged positions, I am also keenly aware of the attraction that feminist ideology holds out for both trans- and cis-gender men operating outside Brahminical–patriarchal reproductive heteronormativity.

While WSCs steadfastly hold on to and insist on the originary subject 'woman', and continue defending its theoretical foundations (Martin 2001), the Indian women's movements, too, have been accused of a similar conservatism. Feminists have critiqued the women's movements for shying away from questions of sexuality, or being unable to think of sexuality outside the domain of kinship (Menon 2012). Queer activists and collectives have also complained that the majority of feminists are indifferent to questions about sexuality, which is pegged as trivial and secondary. In this context, Chayanika Shah writes:

> So far as [the] women's movement has been concerned, we have by and large, concentrated on the rights of those who live by the norms laid down by society.... Women who challenge the very basic norms and structures of how society thinks that women should behave—talking of rights for all these women is a difficult task. Acknowledging their existence could be interpreted as endangering the movements of and for the 'good' women. But feminism is not about maintaining status quo. It is about challenging all oppressive structures of society. (Shah 2005: 151)

Ashley Tellis (2018) points out, through a close reading of debates and letters exchanged between feminist and women's organisations (both autonomous and politically affiliated) that cis-gender lesbian women are usually marked out and separated from the category of woman. He concludes that sexuality is not seen as central to patriarchy within the Indian women's movement, which is deeply heterosexual in nature. Thus, the insistence of mainstream women's movements to cast out the 'lesbian' further limits the category 'woman' (Tellis 2018). The women's movements and the queer movement continued to remain at odds with one another. Tellis further contends that the queer movement, overrepresented by cis-gender gay men, has not had any serious engagement with feminism, often ignoring the struggles and histories of women's movements. Although there has been some solidarity and alliance-building, particularly around litigation on IPC Section 377, transwomen have had no conscious engagement with feminism (ibid.). Sanjay Srivastava (2015) too argues that while the emerging field of masculinity studies questions and critiques power dynamics embedded in caste, class, and race, the same questioning is not directed towards the production of 'male' identity and its associated privileges. Thus, even if there is a strong opposition to sexuality-based discrimination, for instance discrimination faced by a homosexual man deemed 'effeminate', masculinist ideologies are not equally questioned (Srivastava 2015). Despite many crucial studies on the linkages between sexuality and women's studies, the two in practice often do not meet. Judith Butler writes on the chasm between feminism and queer theory, stating: 'Within queer studies generally, a methodological distinction has been offered which would distinguish theories of sexuality from theories of gender and, further, allocate the theoretical investigation of sexuality to queer studies, and the analysis of gender to feminism' (Butler 1994: 1).

The existence of women's studies depends on two questions: First, who is the subject of inquiry? And second, how does one define the category of woman? Both women's studies and the women's movements have, for the most part, assumed a self-evident, already formulated category called 'woman', who can be fully represented as well as be the subject of both politics and knowledge production. Questions about the subject have consistently tormented women's studies, particularly the question of 'which' women. The 1970s and 1980s saw a rallying cry against a universal homogenous 'woman' raised in varying contexts by Black women, women of colour, lesbian women, Dalit women, and transwomen, who have often accused women's studies of 'policing borders'. In the Indian context, class and poverty (rather than caste) were treated as central to women's experiences of patriarchy, and informed much of the women's movements and women's studies in the 1990s.

The insistence of women's studies and women's movements to hold on to a pre-determined category, an *a priori* already-constituted subject stems from the need for a language that allows 'women' to be represented. However, with the growing influence of post-structuralist feminism, the idea that gender is always performative and never given has gained rapid ground. Catherine Malabou argues, 'we must accept the idea that feminism can now be understood as a *feminisme san femme*, a feminism without women. Women as a predicate is no longer an obvious given, if in fact it ever was' (Malabou 2011 [2009]: 6). With such theoretical insights that question the very foundation of the subject, it has become almost impossible to articulate politics that claim to represent a category. Judith Butler argues that the question of the subject is crucial for politics, as

> ...political construction of the subject proceeds with certain legitimating and exclusionary aims, and these political operations are effectively concealed and naturalised by a political analysis

> that takes juridical structures as their foundations. Juridical power inevitably 'produces' what it claims merely to represent. (Butler 1990: 3)

The adherence of women's studies to a stable subject, and thus, a pre-determined, fully constituted 'woman' waiting to be represented, and around whom a feminist discourse can be built, demonstrates a 'turf war', a way to protect its subject of inquiry, and thus its very existence. This border policing stands in conflict with the very philosophy of feminism, and as Butler writes: 'Feminist critiques ought to understand how the category of "women", the subject of feminism, is produced and restrained by the very structures of power through which emancipation is sought' (ibid.: 4). The becoming of a gendered subject requires both an impulsive as well as careful mediation on a cultural reality that is saturated with taboos, norms, and regulations. The existence of already given corporeal styles is produced by regulatory frameworks that a subject must negotiate: thus, both the subject and the cultural framework in which s/he exists engage in a dialect that reproduces gender norms and reanimates them. The understanding that the body is contingent rather than natural or fixed, and that it is a product of a hegemonic, heterosexual culture that sees anatomy/genitals as the defining feature of sexual identity, questions the very binary opposition of the 'sexes' on which the category 'woman' is founded.

While many argue that 'woman' is a political category, and a useful one in fighting patriarchy, one wonders whether it has outlived its political efficacy. The positioning of the 'woman' as a univocal signifier that excludes and represses other gendered experience (re)produces regulatory practices, which in turn (re)produce the bodies that they govern. Thus, to retain the category 'woman' requires a repudiation, which in turn produces abjection, and those produced as abject beings never gain the status of a legitimate 'subject'. On the contrary, their existence acts as a foil in producing the subject. To hold on to the falsity of the category 'woman', then, makes the proponents of women's studies complicit in an act of violence that perpetuates the very system it aims to defeat.

In Lieu of a Conclusion

When one thinks through the different schools/waves of feminism, one striking feature that remains common to all is the commitment to 'emancipation'. While feminism remains rooted in modernism, with obligations to 'empower' women, the notion of empowerment itself has come under a lot of discussion. What are the standards, measures, and values with which one can measure empowerment? Which phallogocentric material and symbolic values are adapted and propagated by dominant groups in society, and then used to quantify emancipation? The idea that centuries of gendered exclusion can now be remedied by integrating women into the labour force, offering them development aid, or including them in institutions and systems of representation has been a dominant trend in most feminist projects. Thus, fundamentally, nothing changes. The role of a Women's Studies Centre would be to open up areas of critical enquiry that may significantly question the very category of 'woman' and the field of signification that constitutes the social, and which 'normalises' and consolidates masculinity and femininity. WSCs can be envisaged as areas where heterogeneous research can be conducted with a focus not only on the status and condition of women, but also on generating knowledge about the production of norms that regulate and govern bodies, and which legitimise particular subjects who come to occupy a tiny margin of the hetero-norm. What are the signification systems that produce the masculine and feminine, man and woman? Thus, the question remains: can women's studies survive and adapt itself to the theoretical insights that question its very subject? Or has it outlived its political efficacy?

Note

1. In my association with the School of Women's Studies, Jadavpur University, Kolkata, that spanned over a decade—first as a research scholar, and subsequently as a faculty—I did not encounter any transperon in the classroom. This is also a commentary on the linkages between education and the transgender community and the latter's exclusion from all kinds of institutional spaces.

References

Bardhan, Pranab. 1994. *The Political Economy of Development in India.* New Delhi: Oxford University Press.

Bourdieu, Pierre. 1984. *Distinction: A Social Critique of the Judgement of Taste.* Cambridge, Mass.: Harvard University.

Brown, Wendy. 1997. 'The Impossibility of Women's Studies'. *Differences: A Journal of Feminist Cultural Studies* 9 (3): 79–101.

Butler, Judith. 1990. *Gender Trouble: Feminism and the Subversion of Identity.* New York and London: Routledge.

______. 1994. 'Against Proper Objects: Introduction'. *Differences* 6 (2+3): 1–26.

______. 2009. 'Critique, Dissent, Disciplinarity'. *Critical Inquiry* 35 (4): 773–795.

Deccan Chronicle. 2019. 'UGC Cuts Funds for Women's Centres'. 20 March. Available at https://www.deccanchronicle.com/nation/current-affairs/200319/ugc-cuts-funds-for-womens-centres.html (accessed February 2024).

Derrida, Jacques. 2003 [1987]. 'Women in the Beehive: A Seminar with Jacques Derrida'. In *Men in Feminism*, Alice Jardine and Paul Smith (eds): 189–203. New York and London: Routledge.

Deshpande, Satish. 2004. *Contemporary India: A Sociological View.* New Delhi: Penguin Books.

Ghosh, Suresh Chandra. 2000. *The History of Education in Modern India, 1757–1998.* New Delhi: Orient Longman.

Harding, Sandra. 1998. 'Can Men Be Subjects of Feminist Thought?' In *Men Doing Feminism*, Tom Digby (ed.): 171–195. London: Routledge.

hooks, bell. 1989. *Talking Back: Thinking Feminist, Thinking Black.* New York: Routledge.

Indira, M. 2006. 'Can Self-Financing be a Viable Source of Resource in Traditional Universities?' *Journal of Educational Planning and Administration* 20 (1): 109–123.

Jain, Devaki, and Pam Rajput (eds). 2003. *Narratives from the Women's Studies Family: Recreating Knowledge.* New Delhi: Sage Publications.

John, Mary E. 2002. 'Women's Studies: Legacies and Futures'. In *Between Tradition, Counter-Tradition and Heresy: Contributions in Honour of Vina Mazumdar*, Lotika Sarkar, Kumud Sharma, and Leela Kasturi (eds): 47–62. New Delhi: Rainbow Publishers.

______. 2008. 'Introduction'. In *Women's Studies in India*: 1–18. New Delhi: Penguin.

Krishna Raj, Maithreyi (ed.). 1986. *Women's Studies in India: Some Perspectives*. Bombay: Popular Prakashan.

Kumar, Ravi. 2006. 'Equity, Quality and Quantity—Mapping the Challenges before Elementary Education in India'. In *The Crisis of Elementary Education in India*, Ravi Kumar (ed.): 13–56. New Delhi: Sage Publications.

Malabou, Catherine. 2011 [2009]. *Changing Difference: The Feminine and the Question of Philosophy*, Carolyn Shread (tr.). Cambridge: Polity Press.

Martin, Biddy. 2001. 'Success and Its Failures'. In *Feminist Consequences: Theory for the New Century*, Elisabeth Bronfen and Misha Kavka (eds): 353–380. New York: Columbia University Press.

Mazumdar, Vina. 2010. 'Emergence of the Women's Question in India and the Role of Women's Studies'. Occasional Paper. New Delhi: Centre for Women's Development Studies.

Menon, Nivedita. 2012. *Seeing Like a Feminist*. New Delhi: Zubaan.

Morrow, Raymond A., and Carlos Alberto Torres. 2000. 'The State, Globalisation and Educational Policy'. In *Globalization and Education: Critical Perspectives*, Nicholas C. Burbules and Carlos Alberto Torres (eds): 27–55. New York: Routledge.

Mukhopadhyay, Subodh Kumar. 1998. *Bangali Maddhyabitta O Tar Manaslok* [The Bengali Middle Class and its Mentality]. Calcutta: Progressive Publishers.

Padmanabhan, C. B., and J. B. J. Tilak. 1986. 'External Financing of Education'. In *Fourth Survey of Research in Education 1983–88*, M. S. Buch (ed.), NIEPA. New Delhi: National Council for Educational Research and Training (NCERT).

Panikkar, K. N. 2002. 'Whither Indian Education'. Presentation to the three-day National Convention Against Communalisation of Education in India. SAHMAT. New Delhi. Available at http://www.sacw.net/HateEducation/panikkarAug01.html (accessed November 2023).

Pappu, Rekha. 2002. 'Constituting a Field: Women's Studies in Higher Education'. *Indian Journal of Gender Studies* 9 (2): 221–234.

Patel, Sujata. 2004. 'Higher Education at Crossroads'. *Economic and Political Weekly* 39 (21): 2151–2154.

Patel, Vibhuti. 2005. 'An Overview on Research for Women's Studies in India.' Report submitted to the Sir Dorabji Tata Trust.

Pathy, M. K. 2003. 'Globalisation: The Threat Perception to Equality of Educational Opportunities'. In *Globalisation and Challenges for Education*, National Institute of Education, Planning and Administration (NIEPA): 226–234. New Delhi: Shipra Publications.

Patnaik, Prabhat. 2005. 'Education and Globalisation'. *Social Scientist* 39 (9–10): 100–111.

Shah, Chayanika. 2005. 'The Roads that E/Merged: Feminist Activism and Queer Understanding'. In *Because I have a Voice: Queer Politics in India*, Gautam Bhan and Arvind Narrain (eds): 143–154. New Delhi: Yoda Press.

Sharma, Kumud. 2003. 'Institutionalizing Feminist Agenda(s)'. *Economic and Political Weekly* 38 (43): 4564–4566.

Singh, Varsha. 2019. 'New UGC Guidelines Cuts Funding for Women's Studies Centres'. *Media India Group*, 20 March. Available at https://mediaindia.eu/society/new-ugc-guidelines-cuts-funding-for-women-studies-centres/ (accessed February 2024).

Skeggs, Beverley. 1995. 'Women's Studies in Britain in the 1990s: Entitlement Cultures and Institutional Constraints'. *Women's Studies International Forum* 18 (4): 475–486.

Srivastava, Sanjay. 2015. 'Masculinity Studies and Feminism: Othering the Self'. *Economic and Political Weekly* 50 (20): 33–36.

Stokes, Eric. 1959. *The English Utilitarian and India*. New York: Oxford University Press.

Tellis, Ashley. 2018. 'Men in Feminism: LGBT and Feminist Entanglements over Masculinity'. In *Men in Feminism*, Romit Chowdhury and Zaid Al Baset (eds): 164–179. London: Routledge.

Tripathi, Amalesh. 1994. *Italir Renaissances, Bangalir Sanskriti* [Italian Renaissance, Bengali Culture]. Kolkata: Ananda Publishers.

8 The Future of Women's Studies, or Women's Studies 'to Come'

Rajlaxmi Ghosh

> Can women exercise authority without mimicking the attitudes of guardians?
>
> Catherine Malabou (2011: 105)

One begins with a set of questions: What, in our contemporary times, is the intellectual charge of women's studies? What are the boundaries that define and differentiate it from other kinds of disciplinary spaces in the universities? How does it respond to multiple and conflicting moments in the mainstream university system? How should we, as scholars of women's studies, explore the different possibilities presented to us? Does the interdisciplinary field of women's studies open up a space for knowledge in male-dominated academia?[1] An inquiry into the current stage of women's studies must address presuppositions on which much of its disciplinary structures are founded. These foundational presuppositions can be attended in terms of multiple and contingent theoretical nuances, which include the sociology of knowledge production, historical study of this interdisciplinary discipline, and a study of its methodologies.

My attempt is not to provide any prescriptive formula for the future of women's studies or even to provide an analysis for a 'proper' future for the discipline. A claim to do 'proper'[2] theory or philosophy presupposes a fixed notion, as if I already know from an *a priori* conceptual mastery how to improve a certain set of theorisations about women's studies and its future. This kind of theoretical affirmation incorporates a commitment that is necessarily bound up with notions of teleology. Theory as established by prevailing doxa is abstract, masculine, and objective, lacking any context, history, culture, and subject, whereas feminism celebrates lived experience. If the criterion of theory is always-already masculinised, how can we (re)formulate these criteria? Can such presupposed 'neat' and 'pure' ideas fulfil the ethico-political urgency of a situation? Can there be any intellectual rigour which is not inscribed by phallogocentric parameters? Gayatri Chakravorty Spivak (1985) in one of her interviews sums up this essential impasse as tools and weapons of struggle. She argues that it is no longer a question of maintaining political purity at the cost of political principle, nor is it simply an issue of embracing speculative principles according to a pragmatic need of the hour. It is a pathway between constantly impure positions—recognising that politics is always-already bound up with what it challenges (including theory) and that speculations are always caught up in different political struggles. Therefore, knowledge production in women's studies is not faced with the binary of pure and impure. All options are bound up by constraints of mainstream orthodox knowledge in diverse ways. There can be no feminist site that is not in some way or the other marked by the constraints of patriarchal power. So, feminist philosophers must accept the implications of a phallic framework, methodological fixity, and its inherent presumptions. The inescapable markings of patriarchal settings are present within feminism as well and determine its effectivity in producing counter-productive ruptures in phallic practices (including those enclosed by the articulation of any speculative move). This is the necessary condition of its effective critique of and movement beyond patriarchy. These speculative gestures are not only the 'groundless ground' under which women's studies becomes recognisable with what it criticises, but also constitute the very conditions by which phallogocentric hegemony can be challenged and resisted. Women's studies works within a categorical economy whose function is the systematic reconsideration of established theoretical canon and the enunciation of rigorous practice or action; at the same time, it is also a kind of practice of its own.

So, the ethico-political task of women's studies is to undertake a permanent critique of any hegemonic notion of feminist theorisation, including those (re)articulated by women's studies itself. Its groundless ground is better conceived as the sphere of constant tussle and negotiation, without any fixed and definitive or pre-planned agenda. As a feminist, I cannot argue for a convenient and clear-cut blueprint to be applied in this interdisciplinary space. Women's studies has now become more self-critical, more cognisant of crucial conceptual and ethico-political investments and thus much more perceptive in its everyday struggle. Let me be very clear that as a feminist scholar, I do not have any aggressive claim of mastery over this interdisciplinary field. There are many modes of theorisation about the future of women's studies and arguments in this chapter are just one of the many arguments about the future of women's studies.

Although disciplines may change over time and new areas of interest emerge, nonetheless each discipline is thought to retain characteristics that separate it from all others. While every disciplinary field focuses on specific areas of investigation, women's studies does not centre on a single issue of gender oppression; rather, it focuses on complex and multiple issues that intersect with gender. One of the most important issues raised in the academic space of women's studies is a call for foundational changes in universities. These changes are not simply about overt attempts to include studies about women in society, but also about seriously considering newer challenges of approaches and methodologies. This increasingly important undertaking demands sustained scholarly attention and deliberation.[3] An inquiry into the current state of women's studies needs to address presuppositions on which its interdisciplinary structure is founded. Law is the basic grounding logic of any institution. Can we say that if an institution is the law, then the guardians of the institution are the guardians of the law? Jacques Derrida addresses this in his essay, 'Women in the Beehive' (1987). We can stretch that argument to ask: What are the risks and chances of the institution of women's studies? 'Do the women who manage these programs, do they not become, in turn, the guardians of the law, and do they not risk constructing an institution against which they are fighting?' (Derrida 1987: 90).

After my preliminary scepticism of my (own) speculative move, I now directly reflect on the main issue of this chapter: the future of women's studies or women's studies '*to come*'. Are those closely associated with women's studies rearticulating the same norms and regulations as other disciplinary paradigms within the university system? Is it primarily filling a lack in the same structure? Is it simply the inclusion of another department in the structure already in place? What then is the significance of women's studies? If the future of women's studies is a mimicry of all other disciplinary practices in the university, can we say that it symbolises the failure of the groundless ground of women's studies? How does one think critically about its future? Are we reproducing the old model of the university, rooted in a Eurocentric paradigm constructed at the beginning of the nineteenth century in Berlin, Germany? All the objects of study which structure the university system of knowledge production today were already established by the nineteenth century, whether literature, philosophy, mathematics, physics, or social science—nothing new, except women's studies. There was no place predicted in this classical model of the German university structure for women's studies (Derrida 1987). Can we do women's studies as mavericks, charting a different course for the field?

There is a clear disparity between what role the interdisciplinary space of women's studies is called upon to play, and its current configuration, which incorporates all kinds of mechanisms of erasures, exclusions, and marginalisation. Its valourisation of the 'thetic', along with its policing, surveillance, and censorship of disciplinary boundaries dissuades any kind of transgression. The necessary task is to conduct research and produce new knowledge—but that does not in itself mean that one is questioning the university system. One is reproducing the same knowledge system, the same exclusions and hierarchies. Whether one knows it or not, one is just repeating the same old phallogocentric model. If the success of women's studies posits only biological women as the sole agents of women's studies, then nothing has changed. It is an inevitable task of the women's studies practitioner not to re-produce the same phallic culture, as this would only be a verbatim rearticulation of the same hierarchical binary system, rather than its displacement. Instead of showing the limitations of phallogocentric knowledge production, such a move just alters the role of the agent of knowledge, strengthening the role in its new form. The structure of the university system remains the same. Women would become the new agents of this phallic knowledge, and their role as mere producers of such knowledge would make them complicit in this structure. Thus, our task is not only to question and critique but to create new concepts for the transdisciplinary field of knowledge production. The threat of collapse of women's studies is the danger of its own success. While there is an ethico-political urgency to speak as women against those who would hegemonise the category 'woman' or deny that such hegemony exists, there is also an internal imperative not to erase, exclude, or suppress the diverse women who are ostensibly represented by the spokespersons of this category. One has to be critically vigilant of the multiple axes of the epistemic field. Women's studies ought to be attentive of circumventing and repeating the exclusionary or hierarchical praxis against which it seeks to respond. It produces knowledge marked by sexual difference, which leads to new potentialities of self-definition and warns us against a humanist politics of merely impersonating men.

Franz Kafka in his parable 'Before the Law' (1971 [1915])[4] suggests that the condition of any institution is law. Every institution is marked by the law. Law produces institution and at the same time institution produces guardians of law. Taking a cue from Kafka's parable, I posit the following questions in the context of the interdisciplinary field of women's studies: Who are these guardians of laws? Do they replicate the kinds of phallo(go)centric rules, regulations, and laws found in mainstream disciplinary practices? There are always such possibilities that subvert the core ethos of women's studies. I do not want to treat women's studies as a ghettoised domain of knowledge in the university; additionally, I am also aware that the university does not have any sort of insular existence in society, and is in fact embedded in societal norms and structures. So my question remains: Does everyone concerned with the interdisciplinary field of women's studies embody phallo(go)centric laws? Does the institutionalisation of women's studies create intellectual boundaries?[5] Most traditional mainstream disciplines are founded through exclusion, erasure, suppression, and illusions about their own stable boundaries. The desire to establish itself as a (mainstream) discipline has invoked in most cases a certain methodological fixity and an excessive specificity that damages and scarifies the discipline's imaginative potentialities, reducing it to some kind of positivism. Therefore, it reinforces the same sociohistorical power it was intended to resist. bell hooks (1984) writes that the means through which universities toil to emphasise and maintain status quo, and the means through which knowledge is fashioned as commodity, leads women's studies to effortlessly turn into a neo-conservative space where radical feminist thinking and feminist activism are submerged or domesticated to the objectives of academic careerism. Without diminishing this problem in any way, our own fight as academics is to attempt to be successful in institutions. Such an endeavour is well-suited with liberatory feminist resistance only when we warily and tactically tie the two.

> When this connection is made initially but not sustained, or when it is never evident, women's studies becomes either an exotic terrain for those politically chic few seeking affirmation or a small settlement within the large institutional structure where women (and primarily white women) have a power base, which rather than being oppositional simply mirrors the status quo. (hooks 1984: 53)

So far this chapter has merely asked some questions regarding the grounding principles of women's studies, but without any clear answer or alternative solution. My project here is not to provide any solution or counter-narrative of phallo(go)centric knowledge, nor do I seek to offer a teleological study of the disciplinary history of women's studies. I am more interested in chalking out the notion of the future of women's studies as radical alterity, as an absolute other. This future '*to come*' of women studies cannot be logically derived from present circumstances. Feminist scholars should interrogate whether the very institutional schemas once put together to support their rich and stimulating cerebral endeavour now work in opposition to it, or run contrary to its most faithful nature.[6] In her essay, 'Feminist Futures', Elizabeth Grosz (2002) writes that a transformative (re)thinking of women's studies is required, which is itself associated with a (re)formulation of the question of institution. Rather than the anarchic abolition of institutions, what we require is counter-institutional inventiveness that would in every instance contribute to some forms of structural impermanence, self-reflection, criticality, persistent alteration, and therefore reflective exposure. 'Each in other words, hopes to assume rather than deny their own deconstructurability, negotiating in their own singular fashion those interminable struggles, at once internecine and heterogenous, that beset the institution as a species of its auto-immune disorder' (Grosz 2002: 15).

To (re)formulate an avant-garde feminist pedagogy, we must abandon our connections with the established traditions of teaching that reinforce hegemony. I must caution that this is a very difficult and complex task. Traditional mainstream disciplines even today regard women's studies as not critically 'academic' and 'rigorous', but as something more concerned with 'personal stuff'. Their courses, perceived as 'gut' classes, have led many feminist academicians to depend further on traditional, conventional pedagogical styles. One must reiterate here that the fundamental substitute to the status quo should never be a simple inversion.[7] That is, being critical of the absence of personal experience in orthodox disciplinary classrooms does not necessarily mean that personal experience should become the key trait of the women's studies classroom. 'Is it possible to radically reconfigure women's studies programs without sacrificing the feminism they promulgate among students and help to keep alive at universities?' (Brown 1997: 97)

Women's studies require some kind of bastardisation, grafting, and contagion. Confrontation with mainstream theorisation cannot be perceived as only external or ahead of the principal order but is conditioned and made possible by it.[8] Derrida asks: '[N]evertheless, if this future is of the same type as that of all other departments, of all university institutions, is this not a sign of failure of the principles of women's studies?' (Derrida 1987: 190).

This chapter connects the disciplinary space of women's studies with a notion of the future as promise and hope of what the future might yet become. Women's studies '*to come*' is a promise for/of the future. One cannot exhaust the radical possibilities of that promise and that hope: It is always '*to come*'. This future is not pre-programmed. It is unpredictable and not determined by *telos*. Derrida states: 'Teleology is, at bottom, the negation of the future, a way of knowing beforehand the form that will have to be taken by what is still to come' (Derrida 1997: 20). For Derrida, the promise of this coming itself is a messianic affirmation that underlines the unconditional promise of a radical exteriority and alterity that opens beyond the totalitarian system.

The Derridean notion of messianic has nothing to do with any messiah with a proper name. It is drawn from an essay by Walter Benjamin, 'Theses on the Philosophy of History'. Benjamin (1992) refers to a 'weak messianic power' that links each of us today to those who came and suffered before us. We are the chosen ones whose current time was once the promised future of the past. Therefore, it is our responsibility to remember and address the injustices that were suffered by those who made it possible for us to live. For Derrida, this is to resignify the present in terms of a never-ending future '*to come*', which is based on our 'inheritance' from the past. This promise of a future '*to come*' is a gift[9] from others who are not known to us. Thus, we have a double responsibility. On the one hand, we have to offer to indefinite others the gift of time to come; and on the other, there is a continuous effort in the present to protect and to build upon the achievements that others bestowed on us. This is the reason for Derrida's insistence that legacy always incorporates 'the work of mourning', and of recalling others of the past who promised us a future in which others (like us) could come 'to be'. Thus, our time today is 'out of joint' with history envisaged as *presence*, because each and every instant of the present day remains entirely open to the spectrality of others. These haunting others are traces and arrivants who never quite take the form of 'historical subjects' with proper names. The messianic coming is not to be confused with concrete presence in recorded history, happening in an everyday time. This messianic is a configuration of experience which signifies something we could not foresee and expect. It is the characteristic principles of the messianic to which we can, and must always, have no choice but to say, 'come'.

Our inheritance consists of today. This very moment, this present is made possible by the past. We must remember this. But within this very moment there is the possibility of a messianic promise of other moments to come. We must never let that promise take the form of a pre-planned future because doing so would close us off from what must be allowed to come unexpectedly. Derrida writes,

> that this messianic remains an ineffaceable mark—a mark one neither can nor should efface of Marx's legacy, and doubtless of inheriting, of the experience of inheritance in general. Otherwise, one would reduce the event-ness of the event, the singularity and the alterity of the other (Derrida 1994: 28).

Marx's inheritance is not reducible to a manifesto for change. For Derrida, we have inherited both from Marx and the Enlightenment tradition the messianic promise of change. The Derridean notion of responsibility toward the future is a promise[10] for the future to come. Thus, we cannot let ourselves be guided by a sense of duty to adhere to present-day agendas. Waiting for the Messiah with a proper name would not transform anything, as what one would be waiting for is the coming of an actual event. Actual events belong to the history of presence, to history as presence, even when they take the form of a spiritual promise. Derrida's radical conceptualisation of an absolutely open-ended future that must always remain to come necessitates an acceptance of having to wait without knowing what we are waiting for, without being conscious of waiting for an absolute event whose coming must be unexpected.

I argue for the *future to come*[11] as a structure of our existence, which involves 'waiting' without any fixed destination and openness toward a future that can never be inscribed by the horizon of significance that we bring to bear upon the possible future. It does not define future that will one day become present, but an openness toward unprogrammed futurity that is (im)possible, entirely ungraspable, and unknowable. Drucilla Cornell writes that 'this future "*to come*", in that it is always what is "to come", is never reducible to what is "yet to come" (as if the yet could be given any form in advance of the event itself)' (Cornell 2005: 68). The relation with singularity of the other is not reducible to any code, system, or formula.

> 'Leaving room for the other' does not mean 'I have to make room for the other'. The other is in me before me: the ego (even the collective ego) implies alterity as its own condition. There is no 'I' that ethically makes room for the other, but rather an 'I' that is structured by the alterity within it, an 'I' that is itself in a state of self-deconstruction, of dislocation.... (Derrida 1997: 84)

So the future to come will arrive before we can foresee it. The future 'to come' is an absolutely unanticipatable arrivant. It finds its very condition of possibility in the radical other.

The future always remains to come, not as a future moment or horizon in itself, at which women's studies will arrive eventually. Instead, women's studies '*to come*' remains and names the responsible encounter with singularity, undecidability, and otherness. The eruption of the other into this reading does not and cannot fit at ease within any explanatory framework by which we demonstrate the possible. One cannot domesticate this future '*to come*' by means of theory. It is an event[12] rather than a concept. So, one cannot offer a fixed trajectory for a new mode of criticism. Women's studies '*to come*' will always surprise us with its singularity and innovativeness. It does not only open itself toward the undomesticated future, but it is inevitably constituted by this openness toward the future-to-come. The future is the experience of the undecidable. Therefore, it cannot come to an end. So, rather that determinism, which necessarily reduces the future to *self-presence*, undecidability needs to be asserted.

Is it possible to reconfigure women's studies without diluting the rigour of feminisms they affirm amongst students and keep alive the programme at universities? Similar to Elizabeth Grosz (2002: 11), Sara Ahmed (2000) too shares a suspicion of 'setting agendas' for women's studies, if this means transforming an interdisciplinary space into a fixed programme wherein it is assumed that an object or goal can always be translated into an outcome. This future-oriented ethico-political move of women's studies not only questions the way in which the world is organised in the present, but also seeks to transform it and engender new modes and forms of living. It is allied with a philosophy of futurity that is tied with flux and instability and indeed, a certain kind of love and respect for radical otherness. Such a philosophy of alterity is one of a hope made possible by the very impossibility of anticipating what is that we might yet become.[13] Being open to the futures that cannot be imagined does not require that we avoid setting agendas and defining our commitment in the present. The question is not so much how not to set agendas, but how to (re)make and (re)imagine the imaginaries of such agendas, and how to allow them to be kept open for negotiations, as well as kept open in the face of transformations in the present that are surprising.

Women's studies *to come* is not a utopia, as utopian logic remains constrained by a chronological thinking of time. Here, I am trying to conceptualise time differently. It does not demand a chronological future—something that we are getting 'closer to' day by day, under the banner of chronological progress. But the messianic experience to which I refer takes place here and now; the fact of promising is an event that is not utopian. This happens in the singular event of ethical embrace. Women's studies *to come* does not mean that tomorrow it will be realised in an actual fashion. Following Claire Colebrook (2010), we can hope for a future which does not have an end and which is always a surplus beyond actualities. For her, hope is the condition of time that is neither sequential nor mechanical—a tendency that opens the present beyond itself. This future of women's studies must be thought under the rubric of the (im)possible. It is not a regulative Idea or Ideal, as the regulative Idea always-already remains on the order of the possible, an ideal possibility that is infinitely deferred. But here I propose a future to come which is not bound by chronology and thus cannot be understood on the register of the possible future. This is why women's studies will never exist in the ontic register in the sense of a present, real existence. It will always remain aporetic in its calculable structure.

Notes

1. This chapter does not deal with the empirical details of the evolution of women's studies, nor is it any kind of ontic study. Rather, its main concern is to dwell on the conceptual difficulties of women's studies as a 'discipline', as well as the challenges of reconfiguring a future, not as a full presence.

2. Here I am referring to the phallogocentric order of propriation (in all its senses of 'property', proper, propriety). See Derrida (1979).

3. Women's studies is not a 'pure' discipline but mediated by multiple singular, contradictory, and contingent moments. Multiple factors inscribe every moment of its articulation in many different ways.

4. See Derrida (1992) for other interpretations.

5. For example, it is always possible that figures of authority in women's studies work in the same manner as those in any orthodox discipline. They would then produce the same codes and conventions, follow the same norms of the mainstream discipline. Thus, it is positions of authority that we should scrutinise and interrogate to see how they are enmeshed with power dynamics.

6. Strategically, it is necessary to speak about the establishment of women's studies, but what next? Law itself can work as hymen, the forbidden place. But we can always use that strategically by subverting the Law from within.

7. Any kind of inversion always only inverts the hierarchy. It reinstates the hierarchy in a new manner, but does not question it altogether. One can sometimes use it as a strategy, but it is still the wrong move. Here, the inversion works in accordance with the dominant. However, I am not proposing any alternative imaginary.

8. Hegemony is not homogenous. It is marked by multiple contradictory moves. See Laclau (1985).

9. In his text, *Given Time, Counterfeit Money* (1992), Derrida argues that the notion of gift contains an implicit demand that the genuine gift must reside outside of the oppositional demands of giving and taking, and beyond any mere self-interest or calculative reasoning.

10. A promise always marks an inauguration: In the act of promising, one promises to inaugurate a process that will lead to the fulfilment of one's promise in a time to come. But that is not a guarantee, and some promises are easier to keep than others.

11. This future to come is not something empirically present. One cannot reduce it to empirics. It works like a gift beyond calculation.

12. For Derrida (2007), an event worthy of the name must be radically singular, irruptive, unanticipatable and, in a certain way, beyond apprehension. An event must overflow its own context and representation. The event must go beyond the realms of an already-possible possibility. The event in its absolute singularity is thus resistant to cognitive description, critical objectification, interpretative reduction and, for that matter, 'theoretical' elaboration.

13. We cannot totally calculate our hope and future. It is beyond calculability, yet at the same time we must work towards this hopeful future. I am not talking about any kind of Hegelian dialectical move here. I am aware of the fact that we cannot totalise and freeze it completely in a full-present moment, yet we have to work with it. We cannot liquidate it to a full-present future. We have to work within phenomenology and be attentive to the aporetic moves inherent in it. Aporia works as an active force here.

References

Ahmed, Sara. 2000. 'Whose Counting?'. *Feminist Theory* 1 (1): 97–103.

Benjamin, Walter. 1992. 'Theses on the Philosophy of History'. In *Illuminations*, Hannah Arendt (ed.): 3–8. London: Fontana Press.

Brown, Wendy. 1997. 'The Impossibility of Women's Studies'. *differences: A Journal of Feminist Cultural Studies* 9 (3): 79–101.

Colebrook, Claire. 2010. 'Toxic Feminism and Hopelessness after Feminism'. *Journal for Cultural Research* 14 (4): 323–335.

Cornell, Drucilla. 2005. 'Derrida: The Gift of the Future'. *differences: A Journal of Feminist Cultural Studies* 16 (3): 68–75.

Derrida, Jacques. 1979. *Spurs: Nietzche's Style*, trans. Barbara Harlow. Chicago: University of Chicago Press.

______. 1987. 'Women in the Beehive: A Seminar'. In *Men In Feminism*, Alice Jardine and Paul Smith (eds): 189–203. New York and London: Routledge.

______. 1992. *Given Time: I. Counterfeit Money*, trans. Peggy Kamuf. Chicago: University of Chicago Press.

______. 1993. *Aporias*. Stanford: Stanford University Press.

______. 1994. *Spectres of Marx: The State of the Debt, the Work of Mourning, and the New International*. New York and London: Routledge.

______. 1995. *The Gift of Death*. Chicago and London: The University of Chicago Press.

______. 1997. 'Choreographies: Interviews'. In *Feminist Interpretations of Jacques Derrida*, Nancy J. Holland (ed.): 89–108. Pennsylvania: The Pennsylvania State University Press.

______. 2005. *Rogues: Two Essays on Reason*. Stanford: Stanford University Press.

______. 2007. 'A Certain Impossible Possibility of Saying the Event'. *Critical Inquiry* 33 (2): 441–461.

Grosz, Elizabeth. 2002. 'Feminist Futures?' in *Tulsa Studies in Women's Literature* 21 (1): 13–20.

hooks, bell. 1984. *Feminist Theory: From Margin to Center*, 49–53. Boston: South End Press.

Kafka, Franz. 1971 [1915]. 'Before the Law'. In *The Complete Short Stories*. UK: Schocken Books.

Laclau, Ernesto, and Mouffe, Chantal. 1985. *Hegemony and Socialist Strategy: Towards a Radical Democratic Politics*, trans. Winston Moore and Paul Cammack. London: Verso.

Malabou, Catherine. 2011. *Changing Difference: The Feminine and the Question of Philosophy*, Carolyn Shread (tr.). UK: Polity Press.

Spivak, Gayatri Chakravorty. 1985. 'Criticism, Feminism and the Institution: An Interview with Gayatri Chakravorty Spivak'. *Thesis Eleven* 10/11 (1): 175–187.

Notes on the Contributors

Arpita Anand completed her PhD in Women's and Gender Studies at Ambedkar University Delhi, offered in collaboration with the Centre for Women's Development Studies, New Delhi. She holds an MA and MPhil. from the same institution. Her research is focused on the disciplinary histories of women's studies, feminist epistemology, and social inequalities in higher education.

Shadab Bano is Professor of History at Aligarh Muslim University. The primary thrust of her recent scholarly work is on women's history, Muslim women's 'reform', and women's education rights. Her writings are on the themes of women's history and slavery in medieval India and women students' struggles against discrimination on campus.

Rajlaxmi Ghosh teaches at the department of Languages, Literatures and Cultural Studies, Manipal University, Jaipur. She is interested in exploring the interface between literature and philosophy. Her fields of expertise are sexual difference, phenomenology, and deconstruction.

Devaki Jain graduated from Oxford and taught Economics at Delhi University from 1963–1969. She has founded a wide range of institutions including Development Alternatives for Women for a new era (DAWN) and Institute of Social Studies Trust (ISST). She has been a member of several policymaking bodies in India and abroad, and has also been a visiting fellow at universities outside India. She was awarded the Padma Bhushan in 2006. Her memoir, *The Brass Notebook* (2020), has been translated into Hindi, Marathi, and Kannada.

Mary E. John is an independent scholar based in Bengaluru and writes on themes related to women's studies and feminism. She was formerly Professor and Director of the Centre for Women's

Development Studies, New Delhi. Her most recent publications are the co-edited volume *Women in the Worlds of Labour: Interdisciplinary and Intersectional Perspectives* (2021) and the book *Child Marriage in an International Frame: A Feminist Review from India* (2021).

Nithila Kanagasabai is Assistant Professor at the School of Media and Cultural Studies, Tata Institute of Social Sciences (TISS), Mumbai. She researches and writes on feminist media studies, feminist pedagogies, journalism studies, academic mobilities, research cultures, digital media, and friendship. She has co-edited the volume *Yaari: An Anthology on Friendship by Women and Queer Folx* (2023).

Panchali Ray is Associate Professor in Anthropology and Gender Studies and Associate Dean (Academics) at Krea University. She has authored *Politics of Precarity: Gendered Subjects and the Health Care Industry in Contemporary Kolkata* (2019) and has edited the volume *Women Speak Nation: Gender, Culture and Politics* (2020). Currently, her research interests include *chars*, borders, migration, and care in Bengal.

Sunera Thobani is Distinguished Professor at the Department of Asian Studies at the University of British Columbia and Fellow of the Royal Society of Canada. Her scholarship focuses on critical race, postcolonial, diasporic feminist theory and practice; colonialism, globalisation, citizenship, and migration; Muslim women, media, and the war on terror; and South Asian women's and sexuality studies.

U. Vindhya is presently an independent researcher, and formerly Professor at the Tata Institute of Social Sciences, Hyderabad campus. Her co-edited volume, *Handbook of International Feminisms: Perspectives on Psychology, Women, Culture, and Rights* (2011) won the Distinguished Publication Award 2012 from the Association for Women in Psychology (USA).

Index